Praise for

The 77 Habits of Highly Ineffective People

"Becoming an ineffective person is easier than you think. Chances are you're already well on the way."

—author of
In Search of Mediocrity

"The 77 Habits of Highly Ineffective People *has provided the blueprint for our corporation. I guess that just about says it all."*

—C.E.O.,
3-Mile Island Nuclear Facility

"This book is so good, I could have written it myself."

—author of
The One-Minute Procrastinator

The 7 Habits of Highly Ineffective People

by Jim Becker, Andy Mayer, and Barrie Maguire

cartoons by Barrie Maguire

Andrews and McMeel
A Universal Press Syndicate Company
Kansas City

 For information, write Andrews and McMeel, a Universal Press Syndicate Company, 4900 Main Street, Kansas City, Missouri 64112.

The 77 Habits of Highly Ineffective People is produced by becker&mayer!, Ltd.

Typesetting by Dona McAdam, Mac on the Hill

Library of Congress Cataloging-in-Publication Data

Becker, Jim.
The 77 habits of highly ineffective people / by Jim Becker, Andy Mayer, and Barrie Maguire ; illustrations by Barrie Maguire.
p. cm.
ISBN 0-8362-1752-7 : $6.95
1. Cost and standard of living—Wit and Humor. 2. Cost efficiency—Wit and humor. I. Mayer, Andrew, 1954- . II. Maguire, Barrie. III. Title. IV. Title: Seventy seven habits of highly ineffective people.
PN6231.C64B44 1994
741.5'973—dc20 93-50210
CIP

Many thanks to Karen Maguire for such an ineffective index.

For Karen

Ineffective habit #1

At least once a day, call your lawyer to chew the fat.

Ineffective habit #2

Send the cat to obedience school.

Ineffective habit #3

Recruit an insurance salesman for your car pool.

Ineffective habit #4

Rely on your sense of direction. (Maps are for wimps.)

Ineffective habit #5

Keep all your valuables (wallet, credit cards, cash, etc.) in your safe deposit box.

Ineffective habit #6

When you need to fax something, call the person first, tell them a fax is coming, and then explain what the fax says.

Ineffective habit #7

Use the speakerphone for phone sex.

Ineffective habit #8

When negotiating with a car dealer, take out your checkbook and say, "I'll take it! How much?"

Ineffective habit #9

Sleep on the job.

Ineffective habit #10

Relax before big meetings by having a drink or two.

Ineffective habit #11

At tax time, wait to be asked.

Ineffective habit #12

Drive all over town looking for the cheapest gasoline.

Ineffective habit #13

When negotiating your salary, tell the boss you'll "be happy with whatever amount he thinks is right."

Ineffective habit #14

Wear your Walkman to your performance review.

Ineffective habit #15

Relocate your compost pile to the kitchen.

Ineffective habit #16

Dress like the boss.

Ineffective habit #17

Increase office productivity by holding daily two-hour meetings on how to increase office productivity.

Ineffective habit #18

Rely on your teenager's good common sense about what time to be home at night.

Ineffective habit #19

Help others communicate better by explaining what they mean.

Ineffective habit #20

Dress for failure.

Ineffective habit #21

Every time that little red light on the dashboard comes on, make a mental note to check your oil the next time you get gas.

Ineffective habit #22

Talk about the boss. Right behind his back.

Ineffective habit #23

If you forget someone's name just call them "Bud."

Ineffective habit #24

Hold your important meetings right after lunch.

Ineffective habit #25

Think up hilarious nicknames for your co-workers and use them often.

Ineffective habit #26

When looking for a man, go where the men are.

Ineffective habit #27

Don't waste time backing up your files—simply print out your hard drive every day.

Ineffective habit #28

Reward yourself for working out at the gym. With a sundae. Or cheesecake.

Ineffective habit #29

Go hunting in a deer costume.

Ineffective habit #30

Guarantee a win in the office Halloween contest by wearing your costume a day early.

Ineffective habit #31

Cut your own hair.

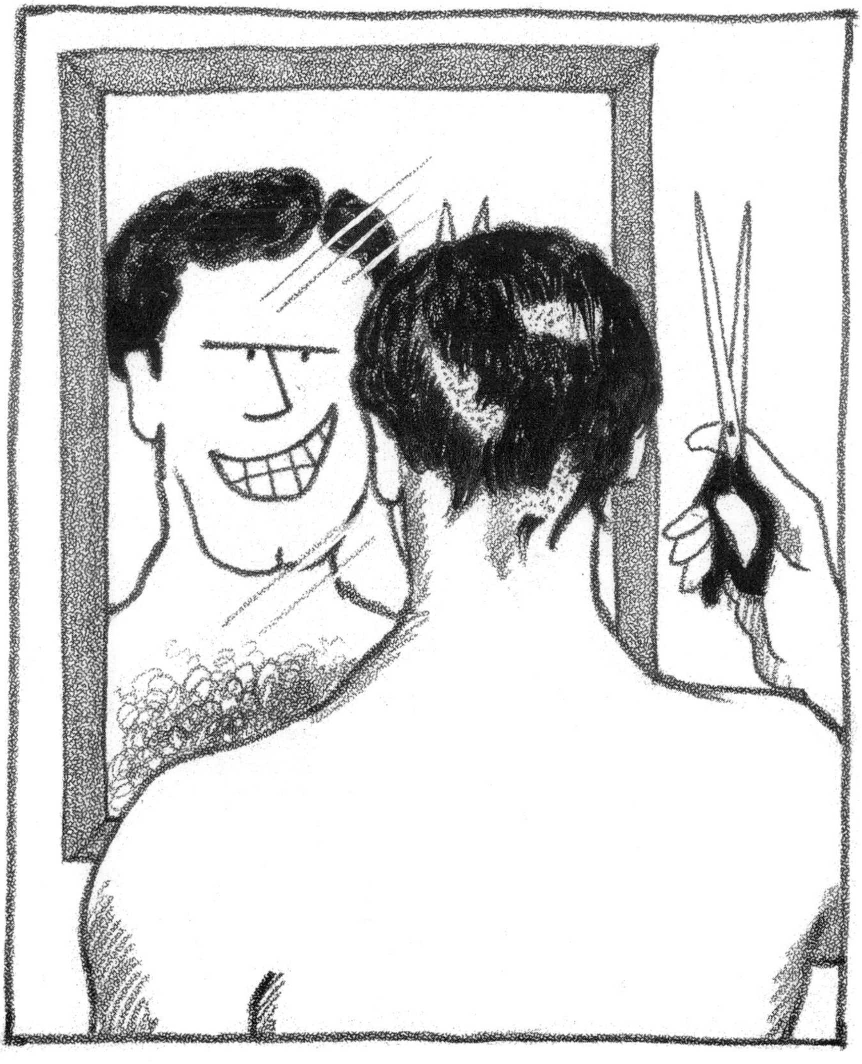

Ineffective habit #32

Whenever you Xerox your body parts, make sure you've got an audience.

Ineffective habit #33

Show the boss your new computer game.

Ineffective habit #34

Always **count to ten before reacting.**

Ineffective habit #35

Maximize your financial clout by keeping your credit card balances at their limits.

Ineffective habit #36

At office parties, humorously say "oink, oink" every time someone picks up a donut.

Ineffective habit #37

Bribe the kids at bedtime by giving them each a liter of Pepsi.

Ineffective habit #38

If you've got it, flaunt it.

Ineffective habit #39

Take your sick days on national holidays.

Ineffective habit #40

Time your phone calls with a stopwatch. (Then, when the bill comes you can make sure the phone company isn't overcharging you.)

Ineffective habit #41

Put *everything* you've *ever* done in your resume.

Ineffective habit #42

Invest in the lottery.

Ineffective habit #43

When you can't remember what floor you want, punch *all* the numbers.

Ineffective habit #44

Give your presentations in mime.

Ineffective habit #45

Keep a spare car key locked in the trunk.

Ineffective habit #46

If it itches, scratch it.

Ineffective habit #47

Study hieroglyphics as a second language.

Ineffective habit #48

When grandparents are visiting, let your teenage son rent a nice movie to watch after dinner.

Ineffective habit #49

As soon as you arrive at the airport, check to make sure you have your tickets.

Ineffective habit #50

If you're quietly circulating your resume, list your boss as a reference.

Ineffective habit #51

Self-treat your bald spot with *real* spray paint.

Ineffective habit #52

Run the grocery list through the grammar-checker.

Ineffective habit #53

Sign your graffiti.

Ineffective habit #54

Don't let state troopers push you around.

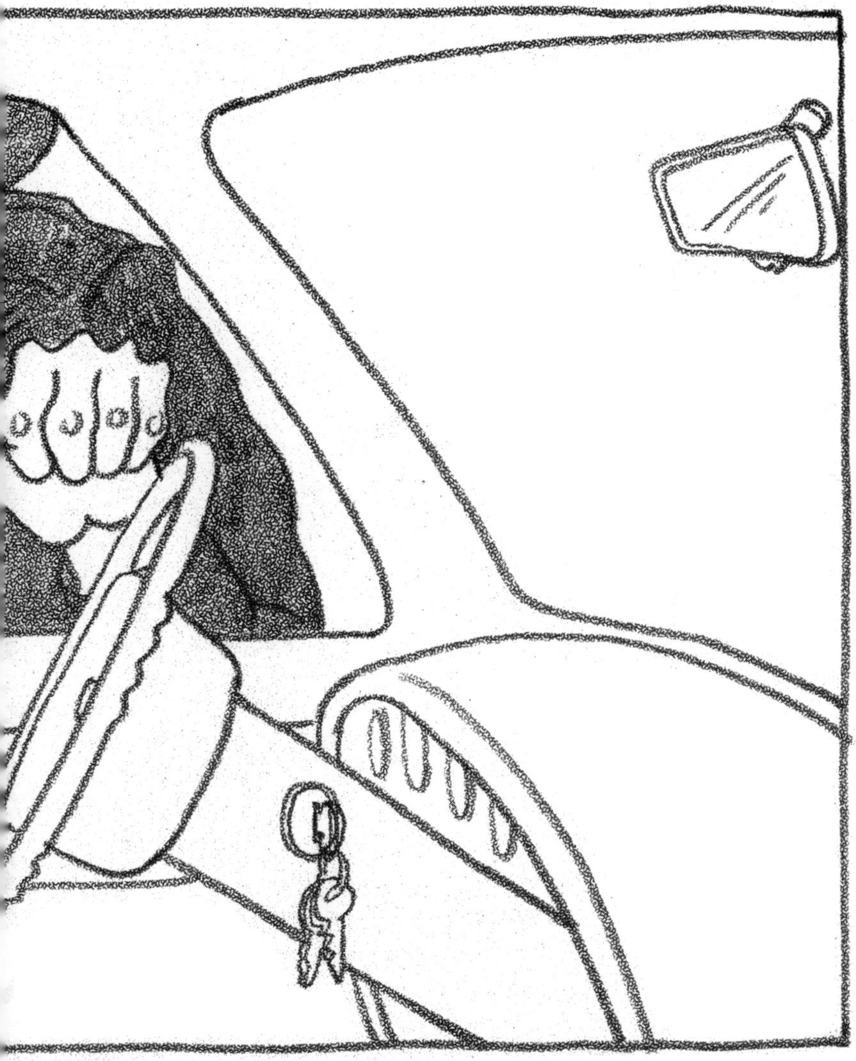

Ineffective habit #55

Let the dog decide how often and how much to eat.

Ineffective habit #56

Shout "I object!" every time the judge speaks.

Ineffective habit #57

Give your performance reviews in the employee lounge.

Ineffective habit #58

Carry several cellular phones.

Ineffective habit #59

Follow up foreplay with a one-hour cooling-off period.

Ineffective habit #60

Floss once a year.

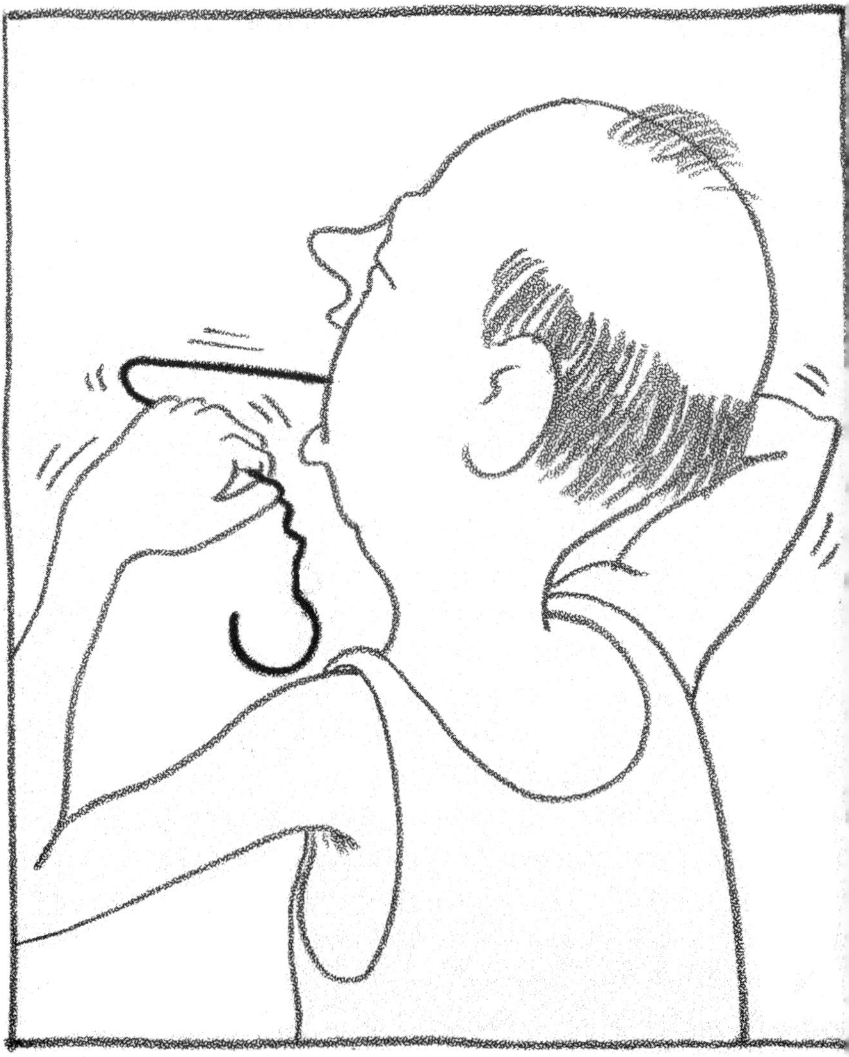

Ineffective habit #61

To lighten your load at dinnertime, let the kids cook dinner.

Ineffective habit #62

For an anniversary gift, buy your spouse a membership at a weight-loss clinic.

Ineffective habit #63

Grab a quick nap a couple of hours before bedtime.

Ineffective habit #64

Top off your gas tank.

Ineffective habit #65

Send your really *hot* love letters by fax.

Ineffective habit #66

Limit your coffee-break conversations to religion and politics.

Ineffective habit #67

If you see a shorter line, go for it!

Ineffective habit #68

Increase your influence over your teenagers (and earn their respect) by lecturing them in rap.

Ineffective habit #69

Hand wash the dishes before putting them in the dishwasher.

Ineffective habit #70

Buy high, sell low.

Ineffective habit #71

To thwart car-jackers, leave "The Club" on when you drive.

Ineffective habit #72

Have your *Hustler* subscription delivered to the office so you can take it as a business deduction.

HUSTLER
MAIL

Ineffective habit #73

Periodically double check your spreadsheet software by working out your profit and loss statement with pencil and paper.

Ineffective habit #74

Buy in bulk.

Ineffective habit #75

Tailgate. (Time is money.)

Ineffective habit #76

Consolidate your debts by paying your bills just once each year.

Ineffective habit #77

Be punctual when it comes to quitting time.

Index

A

advertising. *See* urinal
alcohol. *See* booze
aliens. *See* teenagers
angst, 65
animal nutrition, 40, 60
anniversary. *See* weight-loss
aphrodisiac, 7, 65, 80-81
Arabs. *See* nomad
art
  museum, 52
  office use of, 14-15, 42, 80-81
attorney. *See* lawyer *and* sucker
automobiles
  buying, 8
  care of, 22-23
  carpool, 3
  desert travel and, 4-5
  gas, 13, 22-23, 70
  parts, 22-23
  safety tips, 49, 79, 84-85
  security, 49, 58-59, 79
  vanity plates, 13, 70, 84-85

B

bad credit. *See* debts
bald, 10-11, 14-15, 18, 45, 46-47, 57, 61, 62-63, 64, 66, 74
  fear of, 55
balderdash, 3, 7, 75
ballerina outfit. *See* tutu
ballistic, 28
banana peel, 17
bathroom, 9, 29, 57
bedtime. *See also* hunk
  children and, 41
  napping and, 68-69
beverages, 12, 41. *See also* booze
billable hours, lawyers and. *See* sucker
body parts, 50-51, 71
  breasts, 28, 42
  buns, 34-35
  chest hair, 33, 65
  donuts and, 40
  fingers, 37, 24, 55, 58-59, 62-63, 65, 75, 79
  teeth, 7, 8, 33, 45, 48, 55, 66, 71, 74
booze, 10-11
boss, the
  amusing, 14-15
  companionship with, 24, 36
  computer literacy and, 36
  emulation of, 1
  humor and, 14-15
  resumes and, 54
  ridicule of, 24
box, safe deposit, 6
breasts. *See* body parts
bribery, 41
briefcase, 18, 32, 42, 64, 87
buns. *See* body parts
business
  deductions, 80-81. *See also* sex
  etiquette, 10-11, 16, 18, 24, 26-27, 28, 34-35, 42, 50, 71, 72-73, 80-81, 87
bye bye, 31, 37, 65, 87. *See also* early retirement

C

cajole, 3, 7, 65, 75
camel. *See* dromedary
carjackers. *See* "Club, The"
carnal. *See* it
carnivore, 2, 31, 56, 60, 74
carpool. *See* cars
cars. *See* automobiles
cartoon, 1-5, 7-18, 20-29, 31-42, 44-53, 55-66, 68-87
cat. *See* leash
celibacy, 25, 65
cheap, 13, 33, 43, 78, 83, 84-85, 86
checkbook, 8
cheesecake, 30, 42
chest hair. *See* body parts *and* hair, chest
children. *See also* teenagers
  bedtime, 41
  bribing, 41
  curfews, 19
  dinner and, 67
  parental guidance and, 75
  tasks for, 53, 76-77
chutzpah, 7, 20, 24, 29, 33, 67, 71
circus act, 41
clergy, 25
"Club, The," 79
clue, 4-5, 49
  hasn't a, 24, 28, 37
coathanger, 66
coffee-breaks. *See* confab
communication, 1, 20, 29, 43, 52, 57, 72-73, 75. *See also* hi-tech
compost pile, 17. *See also* odor
computer
  hard drive, 30
  literacy, 30, 36
  printout, 56
  software, 82
confab, 71, 72-73
cop. *See* fuzz
costume. *See* ballerina outfit *and* deer
credit
  bad. *See* bill paying
  card, 38-39
cross dressing, 32
curfew, 19

D

debts. *See* bad credit *and* financial advice
deer hunting. *See* costume
dental hygiene. *See* hygiene
desert, travel in the, 4-5
dinnertime, 67, 76-77
direction, sense of, 4-5
dishes. *See* plates
dishwashing, 76-77
dog. *See* fat
dogma, 3, 72-73, 75
dog-tired, 9, 26-27, 87
donuts. *See* fat
doomsday. *See* truck
drink. *See* booze
dromedary. *See* camel
dun. *See* bad credit

E

early retirement, 24
eavesdropping, 7, 62-63
elderly, sex and violence and the, 53
elevators, 32, 46-47, 64
employee lounge. *See* performance reviews
epicure. *See* gourmet
etiquette
  office, 10-11, 16, 18, 24, 26-27, 28, 34-35, 42, 50, 72-73, 80-81, 87
  prison, 61
  sexual, 7, 65, 71
  shopping, 74

eyeglasses, 2, 3, 10-11, 14-15, 20, 21, 25, 28, 32, 34, 44, 48, 51, 61, 62, 64, 72-73, 81, 86

F

facial hair. *See* hair, facial
failure, 21
fashion dos and don'ts, 18, 21, 33
  plaid, 8, 37, 45, 50-51
fat
  dog, 60
  donuts, 40
  spouse, 67
fax, 6, 71
Feds, the, 12
Fido, 60
film and video rental. *See* information highway
financial advice, 3, 38-39, 45, 78, 80-81, 84-85, 86
fingers, 37, 24, 55, 58-59, 62-63, 65, 75, 79
flim flam. *See* sales
flossing. *See* body parts
food
  animals and, 40, 60
  donuts, 40
  shopping, 56, 74, 83
foreign language, 52
  rap, 75
  travel and, 4-5
foreplay, 7, 65, 71, 80-81
fraternize, 3, 36, 61, 72-73
frown, 4-5, 17, 20, 28, 34-35, 46-47, 49, 50-51, 58-59, 61, 62- 63, 64, 75, 76-77, 79, 80-81
fur, 2, 21, 31, 78
fuzz. *See* Smokey

G

gag. *See* mime
garb, 18, 31, 32
garbage. *See* compost pile
gas, 13, 22-23, 70
geriatric, 53
gourmet, 60
graffiti. *See* poetry
grapevine, 72-73
guns, 12, 31, 58-59
gym. *See* healthclubs

H

habit
  clerical, 25
  ineffective, 1-87
hair
  absence of. *See* bald
  chest, 33, 65
  facial, 2, 3, 31, 57
  styling, 18, 33
Halloween, 32
healthclubs. *See* gym
healthy eating. *See* cheescake *and* sundae
hi-tech, 78
  cellular phones, 64
  computers, 30, 36, 56, 82
  fax, 6, 71
  sex, 7
  Xerox, 34-35
hieroglyphics. *See* mummy
holidays, 43
hunk. *See* stud
hunting, 13, 29, 31, 38-39
Hustler Magazine, 80-81
hygiene
  basic, 50-51
  dental, 66
hype. *See* resumes, sales, *and* sex

I

illness, 43, 53, 60
information highway, 7, 53. *See also* computers
insurance salesman. *See* carpool
interior decorating, 21
Internal Revenue Service, 12
interpreter, 6, 20
investments. *See* lottery
"I object," 61
IRS. *See* Feds, the
it. *See* sex
itching. *See* scratching

J

jail. *See* judge
jailbird, 61. *See also* love prison
job hunting, 44, 54
jokester. *See* quipster
judge. *See* penal system
judgement day, 86. *See also* truck

K

keys, car, 49, 58-59
kids. *See* children *and* teenagers
kitchen, 17, 76-77
kleptomaniac, 38-39

L

labyrinth, 38-39
laugh
  at not with, 14, 24
  dirty jokes and, 57, 71
  world laughs with you, 71, 72-73
lawyer. *See* sucker
leash. *See* obedience
liars. *See* teenagers *and* stud
license plates, vanity, 13, 49, 70, 84-85
lottery. *See* sucker
love
  expressions of, 7, 57, 60
  gifts of, 67
  letters, 71
  poetry, 57
  prison, 65
lunch, 26-27

M

makin' copies. *See* Xerox
mane, 33, 55
mall. *See* debts *and* shop 'til you drop
maps, 4-5
medicine, alternative, 55
meetings, 19, 26-27. *See also* performance reviews
  conduct in, 10-11, 14-15, 50-51
  interruptions during, 34-35
melon. *See* bald
memory tricks, 46-47
milk, 83
mime, 48
movie, 53
mommy, 41, 76-77
mummy, 52

N

names
  forgetting, 25
  nick, 28
  remembering, 25
nap, 26-27, 68-69. *See also* sleep
narcissism, 33, 42
negotiating with,
  boss, 14-15
  car salesmen, 8
  cart, 74
  children. *See* bribe
  judge, 61
  lover, 65
911, 53

nirvana. *See* mall
nitty-gritty. *See* performance review
nomad. *See* Arab
nuns. *See* habit

O

obedience, 2, 75
odor, 17
office
contests, 32
etiquette, 10-11, 16, 18, 24, 26-27, 28, 34-35, 42, 50, 71, 72-73, 80-81, 87
parties, 40
productivity, 19, 36, 43, 48, 82
"oink, oink," 40
outta here, 87
overeat, 40, 60, 67
overhear, 7, 62-63
overwork, 9, 82, 87

P

painting(s)
furs and, 21
head, 55
in office, 14-15, 42
panic, 37
pariah, 72-73
parts. *See* auto, breasts, buns, chest hair, fingers, *and* teeth
penal system, 58-59, 61
Pepsi, 41
performance reviews, 16, 62-63
personals, the, 29
pets, 2, 60
pig, 30, 40, 60
phone sex. *See* sex
plaid. *See* fashion dos and don'ts
plates
cleaning, 76-77
vanity, 13, 49, 70, 84-85
poetry, 57
police. *See* Smokey
politics. *See* religion and
pornography, 7, 34-35, 80-81
presentations, style, 48, 50-51
priest. *See* nuns
profit and loss, 82
punctuality on the job, 87

Q

quaff, 10-11
quid pro quo. *See* lawyer
quipster, 28

R

rain, 49
rap, 75
red-blooded, 7, 42, 80-81
relaxation, 9, 10-11, 58-59
religion. *See* politics and
resumes, 44, 54
resuscitation, mouth-to-mouth, 53
ring and valve job, 22-23
romance, 7, 71. *See also* stud

S

safe-deposit box, 6
salary, negotiating, 14-15
sales. *See also* sucker
car, 8
garage, 78
insurance, 3
salivate, 80-81
scratching, 50-51
scissors, 33
self-esteem, 42, 67. *See also* stud
self-starter, 14-15, 18, 20, 36, 43, 44, 48, 82
sense of direction, 4-5
77 Habits of Highly Ineffective People, The, 58-59
sex
foreplay, 65, 71, 80-81
phone, 7
shop 'til you drop, 38-39
shut-eye. *See* z-z-z's
sick days, 43
sleep, 9, 26-27, 68-69
smell. *See* odor
smiles, 2, 3, 7, 8, 10-11, 16, 18, 25, 28, 31, 32, 33, 34-35, 36, 41, 42, 44, 45, 52, 55, 58-59, 60, 74, 76-77, 78, 83, 86
Smokey, 58-59
speakerphone. *See* sex *and* telephone calls
speeches, assistance with, 20
spouse. *See* weight-loss
stud, 33, 55, 65, 80-81. *See also* hunk
sucker, 1, 8, 14-15, 37, 49, 71
sundae, 30. *See also* fat

T

tailgate, 84-85
taxes. *See* the Feds *and* guns
technique, 7, 29, 31, 65, 71
teenagers. *See also* aliens
curfews, 19
music, 75
video rental, 53
teeth, 7, 33, 45, 48, 55, 66, 71, 74
telephone calls, 43. *See also* sex
cellular, 64
tipsy, 10-11
toilet, 9. *See also* urinal
travel. *See* desert
truck, 37, 83
trunk, 49
tutu, 32

U

unmentionable
umbrella, 49
urinal
advertising in, 29
poetry in, 57

V

valuables, 6
vanity, 42, 55, 65
plates, 13, 70, 84-85
virility, 33, 55, 65
voyeurism, 34-35, 71
vulgar, 7, 32, 34-35, 57

W

walking, 2
Walkman, 12, 16, 75
watercooler, 72-73
weight-loss clinic, 67. *See also* fat
wimps, 4-5
working out, 30

X

X-rated. *See* pornography
Xerox, 34-35

Y

youth, fountain of, 55

Z

z-z-z's, catching some. *See* toilet

Praise for *The Fix*

This novel is more real than most non-fiction, telling a true and painful story about heroin addiction, family secrets, and the impact on children of severe family dysfunction, especially, as is so often the case, when no one talks about what is really going on. In taking her own experiences and crafting a novel, Sharon Leder has done all of us who care about families, children, addiction, and healing a real service.

Ruth W. Messinger, Global Ambassador,
American Jewish World Service

I read *The Fix* cover to cover and wept. I wept as the father of three wonderful daughters. I wept for the young man my older daughter is engaged to marry—a heroin addict in recovery. I wept as a Jew. I wept as a man and a husband. I wept as a politician who knows that between the cold statistics and policy debates about opiate addiction lie millions of personal tragedies about the devastating impact that this crisis is having on individuals, families, and our communities. Sharon Leder tells her very personal journey through the heart and mind of Sara, a young girl coming of age in a family devastated by the struggle of her father, Josef, a heroin addict. In this beautifully written and moving story, Leder shares with us the heartbreak that addiction brings to a family. She does so through the lens of love, innocence, and awakening that moves us to a higher level of understanding and compassion while demanding that we commit the needed support and resources to families in crisis. This is a remarkable book that touches us with despair while inspiring us to action.

Dan Wolf, Massachusetts State Senator

Told through the eyes of young Sara, whose father is addicted to heroin, *The Fix* engages the reader on many levels, creating an affective and touching response. Even today, although drug addiction is more and more in the news, many families and cultures are loath to openly admit their problem and tell their stories. This book is a means to do so, as it presents the devastating effect of addiction from many perspectives, including that of the drug addict, his spouse, his daughter, his parents, and the Jewish community. I could not put *The Fix* down, eager to see if and how a positive resolution would emerge.

Rabbi Deanna Douglas, Rabbinic Advisor, Am HaYam Havurah of Cape Cod; former Director College Counseling, Concord Academy

[redacted]

The Fix does what I would have thought impossible, leading the reader to feel compassion for a man whose decades-long heroin addiction destroyed his life, while almost destroying the lives of his wife and children. Told from the viewpoint of his daughter, Sara, the richness of her love, coupled with the reality of her pain, leads the reader to find a certain nobility in a deeply damaged man. A compelling novel, *The Fix* is also a true story.

C. Fred Alford, Professor and Distinguished Scholar-Teacher, University of Maryland; Author, *Trauma and Forgiveness: Consequences and Communities*

In recovery circles, one often hears the phrase, "You're as sick as your secret." In *The Fix* we watch a child instinctively try to uncover her family's secret and separate her drug-addicted father into two "daddies," one who is sick and another who is loving. We experience the total isolation of a close-knit family, living in an era when the word "heroin" could only be uttered in a hushed tone over a kitchen table, and doing the best they could with the knowledge and resources they had at the time. We travel with a lonely, bright, and giving child as she discovers that her father's "illness" controls not only him but the lives of everyone in her family. And at the same time, we witness her prevailing spirit as it was nurtured by one teacher, who hears her pain and encourages her to express it. Sharon Leder has given us that child's voice with clarity, intensity, and purpose in this moving and important historical memoir, for in the end, *The Fix* isn't about a father's addiction but a daughter's capacity to forgive, heal, and grow.

Beverly Ryle, Career Counselor; Author, *The Field Beyond, A Journey through Family Wreckage*

I enjoyed reading this book because it is written from a child's perspective. In a family, every person has their own interpretation and opinion about incidents and events. Many times children are left on their own to draw conclusions that may not be accurate. The question that families need to ponder is: How much to share with a child and when? This book... can be used as a good basis for discussion between parents who are recovering from an addiction, and children.

Ann Caretti, Ph.D., Director of Student Services, Nauset Public Schools

The Fix

A Father's Secrets,
A Daughter's Search

Sharon Leder

KiCam
PROJECTS

The Preface was published as an Opinion in *The Cape Cod Times,* January 8, 2016. The Prologue was published online as "Private Family Business" in *WIPs Journal* (June 2013). Chapter One of Part One, "Shadow Father," was published as "The Two Fathers" in *Connected: What Remains as We All Change* (Wising Up Press, 2013). Chapter Two of Part Two, "The Lost Father," was published online as "Letter to Mr. Carney" in *Jewish Fiction* (Spring 2014).

Cover and book design by Mark Sullivan

ISBN 978-0-9977222-5-3 (paperback)
ISBN 978-0-9977222-6-0 (e-book)

Printed in the United States of America

Published by KiCam Projects

www.KiCamProjects.com

For Milton who makes all happen

For Ron and Devorah, devoted siblings

In loving memory of my parents, Harriet and George

Contents

Preface ... *ix*

Prologue | 1963 ... *xi*

— THE SHADOW FATHER —

Chapter One | 1955 ... *3*

Chapter Two ... *17*

Chapter Three | 1956 ... *28*

Chapter Four | 1957 ... *37*

Chapter Five ... *51*

Chapter Six ... *58*

Chapter Seven ... *67*

Chapter Eight | 1957—1958 ... *73*

Chapter Nine | 1959 ... *82*

Chapter Ten ... *90*

Chapter Eleven | 1959—1961 ... *102*

Chapter Twelve | 1961—1963 ... *115*

Chapter Thirteen | 1963 ... *126*

— THE LOST FATHER —

Chapter Fourteen | 1963 ... *139*

Chapter Fifteen | 1964 ... *156*

Chapter Sixteen ... *171*

Chapter Seventeen ... *186*

Chapter Eighteen ... *194*

Chapter Nineteen | 1965 ... *199*

Epilogue | 2016 ... *217*

Acknowledgments ... *225*

Preface

In 2001 I moved to beautiful Cape Cod, where I completed my novel about addiction in the Katz family, a fictional name I used to camouflage my own family. I find it ironic that since then, this scenic coastal location has become one of the "heroin capitals" for opiate-related crime. I am also deeply saddened that the rate of heroin overdose in Massachusetts is double the national average. A heroin epidemic now ravages our country, just as one did following World War II, when my own father died of a heroin overdose.

On the evening of December 17, 2015, I attended the preview of filmmaker Steven Okazaki's HBO documentary, *Heroin: Cape Cod USA*. On the screen, I watched eight young adults lay bare their lives as addicts before the camera. The wonderland of sea, sky, and sand that drew me to the Cape to write is the very same place these young men and women became addicted. Initially many of them had access to overprescribed painkillers like Vicodin and oxycodone. But the skyrocketing price of these medications sent the fledgling addicts to the streets of Cape Cod or to nearby Plymouth and Boston for the cheaper heroin now readily available—cheaper ever since Mexican cartels lost the marijuana market in the United States when cannabis was legalized. When the screening ended, four of the eight young "stars" of the film had the courage to speak to the audience in person as part of a panel. We learned that two of the eight had died from overdoses after the film was shot: a young single mother of an infant and a toddler, and a tough-talking young woman who would rather sell her body than steal from anyone to support her habit. We observed a moment of silence in their honor and mourned their loss.

The panel, consisting of the four young addict-survivors, the filmmaker, local and state politicians, and a member of a parent support group, stressed the need for better programs in the schools for early intervention, insurance coverage for longer rehabilitation treatments, and political solutions to counteract the overprescription of painkillers.

One of them said, "Nothing will change unless the public sees the problem."

Another added, "We're great kids who fell into this thing. It can happen to anyone."

When the panel turned to the audience for comments, I was moved to speak because my father didn't have the opportunity to live in these times of greater awareness. I wanted these brave young people to know what a great step they were taking to share their stories publicly. I stepped in line behind the microphone, and told what happened to me in the 1950s and '60s, when heroin addicts like my father had to suffer in secret because the shame went so deep and the stigma could not be shaken.

The Fix is my family's story.

Prologue | 1963

Sara thought of sending a condolence note to Jackie Kennedy. But where should she begin? She was just a sixteen-year-old girl writing to the wife of the president who was murdered. She turned to a blank page in her notebook for Mr. Carney's history class and searched for words.

"How horrible you must feel," she began to write. At once she realized "horrible" was wrong. It was hard to find the words.

"Mrs. Kennedy," Sara started again, "I want you to know that my friends and I at Eastern District High School feel so sorry about the loss of our president, your husband. How sad little Caroline and John Jr. must feel without their father." *Even "sad" was not right*, she thought, and she changed it to "sad beyond words."

Sad beyond words. That's how Sara felt about her own father. He had abandoned her and her family several months ago. Thinking of her father, she couldn't continue the message, and she snapped her notebook shut. *Doesn't Daddy realize how much we miss him?*

Strains of The Ronettes' "Be My Baby" filtered through her bedroom window and lured Sara to the street. She sneaked past the living room where her younger brother and sister, Robbie and Rachel, were glued to the TV screen watching *To Tell the Truth*. Helen, their mother, was dozing on the couch, weary from cooking and serving dinner after a day spent on the icy streets of downtown Brooklyn, where she knocked on doors for J.M. Fields Department Store and encouraged new customers to open charge accounts. No one heard Sara click the apartment door shut before racing down the stairs and onto Penn Street where boys in leather jackets, the ones her smart friends called "rocky boys," listened to transistor radios and leaned against parked cars, smoking Marlboros and kissing tight-sweatered teenage girls. These boys were different from the girl-shy, brainy boys who sat in the honors section of Sara's classes, the boys who argued politics and would sign her letter to Jackie Kennedy.

The girls on the street, the ones clinging to their boyfriends, their eyes darkened with liner and shadow, remembered Sara. They asked where she had been hiding and who she had been hanging out with. The boys coaxed her to smoke. Sara liked the freedom she felt being with this rocky crowd, but she wasn't sure she belonged with them. She felt like a spy, an outsider.

The quiet in the apartment confused Sara when she returned. Most nights Robbie and Rachel kept their mother busy until ten. The buzz of the fluorescent lights under the cabinets drew Sara into the kitchen, where the clock above the refrigerator read 9 p.m.

"Sara Katz!" her mother's voice rang out. Sara's mother sat at the kitchen table, where she had been waiting, and stubbed out her cigarette in an ashtray. "Where did you go? You left without a word."

Sara turned to her mother. "I just went out."

"Where's 'out'?"

"In the street." She shuffled her foot on the linoleum.

"The street? With the dropouts?" Helen reached for a tissue in her apron pocket. "I bet your friend Ruth Taylor wasn't down there wasting her time. She listens to her mother. Mrs. Taylor knows that gang is no good. What's gotten into you? You're student vice president of your school. Don't spoil everything you've worked hard for."

Sara looked down. She had violated their unwritten contract. On weeknights, if she stayed home after completing her homework, she'd be relieved of kitchen chores. That was their agreement. Helen said she wanted all her children around her in the evenings, now that their father was gone. Yet Sara hadn't expected her mother to get so upset.

Glancing at the dinner dishes piled high on the drain board, Sara felt a twinge of guilt. "I was just...going out for air. That's all."

"Sara dear," Helen said, looking bewildered, "you know you shouldn't be hanging out with that loose crowd. You don't want your teachers losing confidence in you."

Sara found her voice. "You think I'm still a child. But I'm not! I need my freedom. You seem to have no faith in me at all."

"I have great confidence in you, *mamela,*" Helen said—using the Yiddish word for "little mother"—"and I want you to do better, do more than I did." Helen wiped her brow and gave Sara a hug. "Your talents I never had. My worst fear is to speak in front of an audience, my voice cracks so badly, but you give speeches at school and express yourself so well. Please don't be distracted by boys the way I was. Forget those roughnecks in the street." Gently she touched Sara's cheek. "You never cared for them before."

Sara looked into her mother's eyes. "Ma, don't worry. I won't be distracted." She gazed at her parents' sepia wedding photo on the kitchen desk: Helen's long brown hair, heart-shaped face, hazel eyes, and full lips; Josef's vibrant eyes, dark, wavy pompadour, and thin moustache. *How perfect they looked! Like two movie stars,* she thought. From 1941 until the end of the war in 1945, the gilt-framed photo sat in the window of Chester Studios on Bedford Avenue, her mother always boasted. Now forty-one, Helen kept her hair short; Josef, a year older, already had gone bald.

Her parents' separation last April had startled Sara and made her restless. Because her father's "problem" was becoming worse while he lived at home and the neighbors might learn about it, Sara's grandparents had decided, against her mother's wishes, that Josef should live with them in Queens and leave Helen and the children in Williamsburg, in the apartment building her grandparents owned. Grandma Hannah and Poppy Mo believed *they* were the only ones who could straighten out their wayward son. How they could fix him, Sara didn't know. In the meantime, Sara promised her mother she would never talk about her father's troubles to anyone, not even to her best friend, Ruth, whose family, Poppy said, were the only *shvartzes*, Negroes, to whom he'd ever rent an apartment. But it was the Jewish neighbors Grandma and Poppy wanted to hide Josef from. They didn't want to expose their *shandah*, their shame, to the old-timers, who, like them, had fled pogroms in Russia and Poland. And they didn't want the *greenhorns* to know anything about Josef's problem either, greenhorns being the younger Orthodox families who had escaped Hitler from Hungary and Romania.

Though Poppy and Grandma had moved to Queens, Poppy still had almost daily contact with his former Jewish neighbors in Williamsburg because they had begged him to keep his butcher shop open, the one he and Grandma had run for more than two decades on Bedford Avenue. They were his loyal customers and wanted to continue to purchase their kosher meat and poultry only from him. And where else, they argued, could they find the delicacies Grandma prepared, like her spicy *kishka*, stuffed derma, and *helzel*, stuffed chicken neck?

When Grandma and Poppy saw firsthand how deeply sick Josef was, they accused Sara's mother of causing their son's problem, and they no longer invited Sara's family to visit them in Queens. Sara couldn't understand how the grandparents she had loved could possibly think her mother was responsible for her father's illness. Her mother took their shunning greatly to heart. She couldn't get over their rejection. She began to smoke constantly and developed a persistent cough that caused her embarrassment, especially when she was tense and tried to speak.

Every Sunday, Sara, Robbie, and Rachel saw their father when he visited their apartment. He would drive from Queens to Williamsburg, checking in first on Poppy's butcher shop and then on his own business, Katz and Block Wholesale and Retail Kosher Meats, on nearby Lee Avenue. His trip was complete with his visit to his family on Penn Street. After seven months, he seemed to be getting better and was always smiling. But Sara wondered, *Was he really getting better, or was he just pretending?* He had fooled them in the past, again and again.

Each week he would arrive laden with gifts—kosher chicken and steak from Katz and Block; *babka* and *rugelach* baked by Grandma; and brightly colored caps, scarves, and shirts he purchased from the Lee Avenue shops near Katz and Block. He liked to entertain his children by playing sad, jazzy tunes on his harmonica. His blue eyes would glisten and roll, and his cheeks would puff and quiver. These moments were precious to Sara. They also seemed to revive her mother's hopes that life could become normal again. Sara couldn't grasp why, over the years, none of the procedures her father underwent had cured him. But now that he was living with his parents, he was going to a clinic in Harlem. *He's doing a lot of apologizing to Ma and us kids,* Sara thought. *Maybe he really is getting better, and I can finally have the heart-to-heart talk with him I've wanted to have for so long.*

The morning after her mother's admonitions, Sara, who was short for her age, had to stand on tiptoes to see herself in the bathroom mirror. She teased her brown hair into a high beehive and slipped on a new blouse, a gift from her father. How she missed him! She preened in the mirror, admiring the blouse, its sheer fabric and its color—her favorite, powder blue. It matched the gray-blue of her father's eyes, and her eyes, too. Considering whether to wear a slip, she remembered the bold Italian girls on Penn Street and draped a navy scarf over her shoulders instead.

Sara thought about the talk she would give at the school assembly later that morning. As vice president of Eastern District's General Organization, she would deliver remarks about the holiday fund drive. She planned to add a tribute to President Kennedy, whose assassination a few days ago had brought the nation to tears and moved her so deeply.

At school, walking down the hallway, Sara was gabbing with Ruth, who often spoke up at assemblies for the Negro students at Eastern District. Larry Roth, the G.O. president, was strolling with them when Mrs. Sherman intercepted the trio. The students referred to her as "the Sherman tank."

"Miss Katz!" the hefty woman barked. "Put your books down. Let me see what you're wearing."

Sara nudged Larry to hold her books. He stood there with Ruth, both witnesses to Mrs. Sherman's scrutiny of Sara. To Sara's distress, the scarf slipped off her shoulders. "No one's delivering a talk for the G.O. dressed like that, Miss Katz."

Sara felt humiliated receiving a reprimand in front of her friends. She looked down at her blouse and averted her eyes from Mrs. Sherman's dagger gaze. Sara couldn't find words to answer. She realized she had taken a risk in wearing a see-through blouse, but she liked the way she looked in it, and her father had given it to her. Should she be blamed for her scarf falling off?

"Mr. Roth, *you* proceed to the auditorium," the Sherman tank fired. "I want you to deliver the remarks for the fund drive. Miss Katz needs me to escort her to the principal's office." She glanced at Ruth, appearing not to recognize her. "Are you a friend of Sara's?"

"Yes, ma'am." Ruth's large, dark eyes met Sara's. "I'm the representative for the Dignity Club, Mrs. Sherman."

"Oh, of course," Mrs. Sherman said, looking at Ruth more carefully.

"See you tomorrow," Larry mumbled, returning Sara's books.

"Don't forget about President Kennedy," Sara said to him over her shoulder.

Sara was sent home for "indecent exposure." Because her mother was still at work, Sara was left with her Aunt Annette, who lived around the corner from the Katzes. Annette phoned Robbie's school and told them Robbie should take Rachel directly to her house in the afternoon—Sara wouldn't be picking them up.

"I don't want to contradict anything your mother has to say," Annette said to Sara. "After all, I don't have a daughter, and your cousin Ben is only ten." Seemingly at a loss for what to do, she ushered Sara into her kitchen and looked nervously through her pantry. Finally, she offered Sara milk and cookies and said they'd wait for her mother.

When Helen got home and learned of Sara's discharge from school, she told Robbie and Rachel to do their homework in the bedroom and led Sara into the kitchen. "Why can't I get through to you?" She looked down at the blouse Sara's father gave her and pointed her finger. "I can see your…your…rosebuds. Don't you realize you have to cover yourself up?"

"I'm not an Orthodox Jew, Ma! Why should I be ashamed of my breasts? Can't you even say the word?" Sara looked directly at her mother for an answer.

"Sweetheart," her mother responded. "All girls need to be modest. You don't want to be considered a tramp."

"I know the girls they call tramps," Sara replied. "I feel sorry for them. They're just girls who want to be loved."

"What am I going to do with you?" Her mother shook her head. "The world may not be fair to those girls, but it's a world we have to live in."

"President Kennedy believed we could make the world different. He created the Peace Corps."

"The president was such an unfortunate man," her mother said. "*Nisht-ugadacht!* We shouldn't know from it! But you need to forget the world right now. Charity begins at home. How about bringing peace to your own family?"

"But Daddy gave me the blouse."

"Your father doesn't always use good judgment."

"He trusts me more than you do."

A silence settled between them. Steam hissed up from the radiator. "There's something else I'm worried about." Her mother began wheezing. "Remember—I don't want you telling your friends about your father's situation." Her stern look drummed home her admonition. "Even the appearance of wrongdoing can ruin his reputation. Don't shame your family. Don't say anything."

"OK," Sara grumbled. "I already told you I wouldn't tell anyone anything."

Sunday arrived, and the children waited for their father's visit. They expected to see him by three in the afternoon, but he was late. Huddled together sadly on the couch, they watched images on TV of the president's assassination. The president and Jackie were in the backseat of the gunmetal gray convertible limousine. They saw Jackie climb out of her seat and onto the trunk of the car after the president got shot.

"I loved the president," Sara said. "Who would want to kill him?"

Eight-year-old Rachel pointed to a man on the screen who was running on the downtown Dallas lawn beyond the motorcade. "It's him! The killer. That man!" she shouted, trembling. Sara calmed her with a hug.

As evening fell, Robbie turned the channel to Disney's *Wonderful World of Color*. He leaned his arm over his new telescope, the *bar mitzvah* gift he recently received from his father. On the coffee table, in preparation for his father's visit, he lined up the airplane models he and his father had assembled on previous Sundays. Rachel, who'd been hoping her father would buy her a puppy, lay on the carpet, her eyes drowsy, petting her cat, Whiskers. Helen prepared dinner.

When Walt Disney ended, Robbie said to Sara, "It looks like Daddy's not coming." With disappointment etched on his face, he switched channels to *The Ed Sullivan Show*.

"He'll be here," Sara said. "He promised."

The phone rang. "It's Daddy," Rachel squealed and jumped up from the floor. Whiskers fled behind the couch. The three children moved away from the television. They gathered around their mother in the kitchen as she lifted the receiver off the hook. Sara knew by the drop of her mother's head that it was bad news.

"God in heaven," their mother groaned quietly. "The butcher shop? No, this can't be. Impossible!" Mechanically, she replaced the receiver. Her face was ashen. She gathered Sara, Robbie, and Rachel in her arms. Her body shook, and she placed her hand on her heart. "That was Uncle Irv," she said, her voice quivering. "Calling...about your father." She hugged the children too tightly. "Something horrible..."

Even in the kitchen Sara could hear the beat of the June Taylor Dancers performing that night on Ed Sullivan. They sounded now like the hoofbeats of horses.

"What is it? What is it? What is it?" Sara yelled.

Helen walked slowly toward the living room to shut the television off. "Daddy had an accident in Poppy's butcher shop," she whispered. "A very bad accident."

The first time Sara saw a corpse, it was that of her father laid out for his funeral on Bedford Avenue. The satin-lined mahogany casket was not open to the public but sat in a side room for the immediate family to view before the service. Sara's mother, dressed in black, wore a veil to cover her swollen eyes and tear-stained face. Robbie, in his *bar mitzvah* suit, stood close to Sara, who wore a dark blue dress.

When Sara saw her father's gray-blue eyes staring up blankly out of the coffin like a mannequin's, his face wan and rigid, she didn't recognize the father she knew—the father with rolling, lively eyes, the one who visited them on weekends, played his harmonica, and sought forgiveness, the father who, over the past few months, delivered packages of meat to the family to prove how much he loved them. Grandma had insisted that Hirsch and Sons, the funeral directors, keep Josef's eyes open for a while, since she wasn't ready to accept that her son was really gone. It was one of the departures from tradition that Rabbi Korn reluctantly allowed to please Grandma. The Conservative Jewish rabbi had been stunned by Josef's premature death and sympathized with Sara's grandmother, who was crazed with grief when she saw her dead son's body—his leathery skin, seal-gray face, and blue lips. Now, seeing her father's face in the coffin, lifeless beyond recognition, Sara thought it was best that her mother and grandmother had not given in to Rachel's desire. Together they followed common Jewish practice and decided she was too young to attend the funeral.

Sara simply couldn't believe her father was no longer alive. There was so much she wanted to talk with him about, and now she would never get the chance. Every day there seemed to be new questions on her list, questions about boys; about what college she should attend, since she was hoping to go out of town; about why the president got shot and why there had to be racism and wars.

As Sara sat between her mother and brother in the pew designated for them, she began to cry softly so her mother wouldn't hear her. She turned to Robbie and said audibly, "I can't believe it. Daddy was just with us at your *bar mitzvah*. And now he's gone."

Robbie bit his lip.

Sara watched the mourners file into the chapel. Her grandparents hobbled to the pew in the first row in front of Sara's family, appearing purposely to ignore them. Her grandmother moaned in agony and seemed to gasp for air. Aunt Rozzie, her father's sister, followed with her husband, Uncle Irv. Their children, Sara's cousins, stared at Sara and Robbie as they passed their row and joined the grandparents. Now Sara's sorrow mixed with anger. *I should also be sitting in the first row, Ma and Robbie with me! We're immediate family. Couldn't Grandma and Poppy put their blame aside so the whole family could sit together? How did they ever convince the rabbi?* And in the row behind Sara, Aunt Annette, Helen's sister, and her husband, Uncle Nat, squeezed into their seats along with their son, Ben, who tapped Robbie on the shoulder when he sat down. "Keep your hands to yourself, Ben," Annette said in a hushed voice.

Sara drew close to Robbie, sobbing. "Daddy's life is over. Things won't ever be the same." Robbie began sniffling. His lip was turning white.

Unable to control herself, her voice rising, Sara tugged Robbie and wailed, "Who is that pretender, that corpse lying in the casket wearing Daddy's favorite gray silk suit?"

"Daddy looks like that because I think he's embalmed," Robbie cried.

"Shhh. The rabbi's ready to speak," Annette whispered from behind.

From the *bema,* the pulpit, Rabbi Korn, bearded and solemn, began speaking. Looking around the chapel, he said, "Friends, we are gathered today to face a modern tragedy.

We remember Josef Katz, the son of Mo and Hannah Katz, our beloved kosher butchers, formerly of Williamsburg, now of Little Neck." The rabbi glanced in Grandma and Poppy's direction, then moved his eyes, row by row, to the very back of the gold-colored room adorned with dark draperies. He seemed to be seeking out familiar faces. Sara could see him perspiring. She wondered if the rabbi, who had known her father since he was a child, had been trusted with her father's secret.

"We begin with the recitation of psalms in honor of Josef, his good life, and his memory that will be for a blessing."

Sara turned to her brother. Cupping her hand over her mouth, she whispered, "How do *you* think Daddy died?"

Robbie looked up at his sister with fear in his eyes. "No one told me." All he knew came from Sara, and the information she had offered was sketchy. "Did Daddy…do it…to himself?" he asked.

"You know about things like that?" Sara asked in surprise. He nodded.

Sara hugged her brother, pulled him closer, and whispered, "We just don't know. Maybe we'll never know. I asked Ma, but she wouldn't answer me. Maybe she doesn't know herself. Ma and Grandma didn't want an autopsy."

Robbie began crying.

"What are you saying to Robbie?" Sara's mother asked, yanking Sara's shoulder.

Sara tried to keep her voice down during the rabbi's reading of psalms, but she wanted answers. "Will Rabbi Korn say anything about Daddy's illness? His struggle to get well?"

"We'll discuss it later. Just be quiet."

At the conclusion of the psalms, Rabbi Korn called family members to the *bema* who wished to speak about the departed. No one came forward. Sara wondered why no one wanted to say anything. *How is it possible? Most people in the room know Daddy.*

Grandma Hannah heaved with sobs in the first row. Though Poppy Mo tried *shushing* her and holding her in his arms, Grandma couldn't contain herself. She cried out, "Josef, my beautiful son, my Josef." Members of the congregation, second cousins from Russia and Poland, broke out in expressions of sympathy:

"Poor Hannah! Her second son, gone."

"God forbid she should suffer a stroke and collapse!"

"A mother never gets over such losses."

"Daddy had a brother?" Sara asked her mother.

"Yes, Alex. He died when he was six," Helen whispered. "Before your father was born."

"Alex? That name sounds familiar. Why didn't Daddy ever talk about Alex?"

"Because Grandma doesn't like talking about him. He was run over by a trolley, and she blames herself for..."

Helen was interrupted by Rabbi Korn, who raised his arms to calm the crowd. Grandma turned to Sara and Robbie seated behind her and asked, her eyes wild, "Why did your father have to die from a heart attack? Why did he have to leave us Sunday morning to go see you?" Poppy coaxed her to turn around.

Sara squirmed in her seat. She had been privy to previous conversations between her mother and grandmother, and she knew that her father didn't die from a heart attack. She leaned over to her mother and whispered, "How can Grandma lie like that?"

"She's not telling the truth because the truth is shameful," her mother answered in low tones. "Daddy's life was shameful, a *shandah*. So was his death. So please keep quiet, Sara. The rabbi's trying to speak."

"His whole life? You know that's not true."

"Quiet now, Sara. This is not the time."

Sara wondered how her mother could expect her to remain quiet. Was a funeral supposed to be like this—no words expressed about her father's problems or the real reasons he died? It was as if her father had been taken from her too many times: Illness took him from her first. Then her grandparents stole him and kept him in Queens. Death, maybe even suicide, took him a third time, and now the rabbi was describing a father different from hers. *Did the rabbi's eulogy have to be such a cover-up? Couldn't he acknowledge who my father really was?*

Rabbi Korn continued: "Josef Katz, loyal son of Mo Katz, carried on his father's trade and branched out far beyond the neighborhood. He brought wholesale kosher products to the entire city. But despite Josef's good intentions, Hashem, the Master of the Universe, revealed another plan for Josef Katz."

Grandma Hannah's deep-throated moans pierced the chamber. Sara looked anxiously about her, at the whole congregation, at the faces of all the people gathered, the relatives, the friends, the acquaintances. *Many of these people*, she thought, *must have known about my father's sickness.* Rabbi

Korn reached the end of his eulogy: "The life of our friend and neighbor Josef, a man fortunate to have a lovely wife and three loving children, was cut off so tragically at forty-two. Oh, who can honestly say that our Josef Katz was not a hardworking, good-natured man? We hold him in our blessed memory, and we thank Hashem that at least in our Josef's brief life he had the *nachas,* the pride and joy, to see his son become a *bar mitzvah.*"

Sara knew better. Her father's tragedy wasn't simply dying young. "What is the rabbi talking about?" Sara asked her mother. "Are we fortunate that Daddy died so soon after Robbie's *bar mitzvah*? That he wasn't even living with us? Why isn't the rabbi telling the truth?"

"Because what happened to your father is private, family business," her mother answered. "So please, Sara!"

Sara moved from feeling disbelief over her father's passing and the untrue ways he was being described to feeling overwhelmed by sadness and loss. No more hope for reconciliation between her parents. No more watchful waiting for the blare of her father's car horn when he drove in from Queens, no more anticipation of her father's step at the door, or his bear hug when he greeted her. Never in the past could she speak to her father about what she knew—his shameful life. Never could she find the right words, the right time. She had imagined approaching him that very week. And now it was too late. If only he had stayed at home and not moved in with Grandma and Poppy, he might still be alive. She cried out uncontrollably to her mother, "Oh, why did Daddy leave us?"

Helen put her arm around Sara, and Sara welcomed her soft touch. She rested her head on Helen's shoulder and wondered what would become of them. Would they have to move out of Poppy's building now that her father was gone? Where would they go? If they remained in their neighborhood, would their Orthodox neighbors spurn them if their father's secret became known? Despite her mother's comfort, Sara's stomach began to knot. Anger welled up in her—anger at her father for leaving them and anger at the lies she had heard. She sat stiffly until the service ended.

Sara returned to classes after the *shiva,* the weeklong mourning period. Mr. Carney, her history teacher, a burly disciplinarian, asked Sara to talk with him privately at his desk.

"*Gurl,*" he said in his brogue, "did you read the chapters on the two world wars and on Roosevelt and the Great Depression?"

At that moment, Sara wished she were back in Miss Simmons' history class during the previous semester. She wished her parents hadn't split apart. She wished her father hadn't had his fatal problem. She wished her father had been cured. She wished she could have spoken to her father about his problem and that he hadn't had to die. She tried to explain all of it to Mr. Carney.

"No, I…my father…my father…" she began. Her heart thumped. Her face felt hot. She trembled. She held onto the corner of Mr. Carney's desk.

"What about your father?"

There was much in her heart she wanted to say, but strangled by the secret she had buried, she stood mute.

The Shadow Father

Chapter One | 1955

"No. It's not true! Shooting up heroin? Josef and Spencer? Impossible!" The screams—Sara's mother's—came from the kitchen.

What's "heroin"? Sara wondered. It was a word she had never heard before. *Is Spencer someone bad?* Sara, eight years old, had just arrived home from Public School 16, holding her younger brother's hand. She settled him down on the rug in the living room, where drawn blinds kept the room dark in the afternoons. She turned up the volume on the TV set and changed the channel to *The Merry Mailman* and rushed into the kitchen. The aroma of stuffed cabbage filled the room. When she saw her mother holding the phone and trembling, she stepped inside the kitchen and shut the swinging kitchen door behind her.

"Why should I believe you?" Helen shouted angrily into the receiver. The ladle she was holding in her hand dropped to the floor. She didn't bother to pick it up. "My husband's not an addict! Do you hear me?" Slamming the receiver down, she collapsed into a chair. "No, he wouldn't do this to me."

Helen looked more bewildered than ever before, even more upset than when Josef began working on Saturdays.

"Mommy, please," Sara begged, grabbing her mother's arm. "What's wrong? What trouble is Daddy in?"

"No trouble, sweetheart," Helen answered feebly, stroking her daughter's hair. "It's just that this call gave me a bad headache. That's all." She stood up, walked to the stove, and turned off the flame under the cabbage.

The phone rang again. With her head in her hands, Helen said, "Let it ring, Sara."

"But it could be Daddy!" Sara cried, picking up the phone.

"I must tell you, Helen," the frantic voice on the other end insisted. "If the police find Josef with marks on his arms, he's finished. They'll arrest him. But if Josef stops, Spencer will stop, too. Spencer's always looked up to your Josef."

"Who is this?" Sara asked, frightened. "Mommy, there's a lady on the phone talking about the police catching Daddy with marks on his arms."

"I told you not to answer it!" Helen snatched the phone from Sara. "Mitzi, don't you ever call here again, or I'll have the police arrest *you*. How dare you spread your hateful stories to my daughter!"

Helen hung up the phone, lost her balance, and held onto the kitchen table to steady herself. She mumbled words that trailed into what sounded like babble to Sara—words about Josef having given up the clubroom gang and the Moonglow boys before the war, before she and Josef got married.

"None of those Moonglow boys still live in Williamsburg," she whispered. Sara didn't understand what her mother was saying. "None of them..." Her lips turned down. "Except for Spencer."

Sara was curious to know who Spencer and the Moonglow boys were, what heroin was, and what marks on the arm meant, but seeing her mother so distraught, she was afraid to ask. Helen paced around the room, cursing Spencer and calling him a good-for-nothing. She muttered to herself as if Sara weren't there, saying Spencer worshipped Josef blindly when they were teenagers and then got himself hooked.

Sara hung on every word.

"I could murder Spencer!"

If only Mom would calm down, Sara thought, moving toward her mother. She took her mother's hand and squeezed it.

"I'll be all right, Sara. Where's your brother, honey?"

"Watching *The Merry Mailman.*"

Helen walked to the living room. "My angel, give Mommy a hug."

Robbie looked up from the TV screen and ran into her arms.

"You be a good boy," she said, twirling some strands of his blond hair. "Play with your sister after your show is finished. You've got blocks and board games. Mommy has to take a little nap."

Searching first his mother's face, then Sara's, Robbie answered, "OK, Mommy." Helen kept her arms around him for a few moments. Then she walked to her bedroom with Sara, who watched her shut the blinds, take the phone off the hook, and grab a Chesterfield cigarette from her nightstand. Helen checked on Rachel, the baby, who was curled up in the crib beside her bed. "I'll lie down...just for a few minutes. Honey, please play with Robbie."

"What's heroin, Mommy?"

Helen's eyes dropped. She was silent for a moment. "Heroin is a dangerous medicine that can make you sick. Your father's too smart to take it."

"A medicine makes you sick?"

"Sweetheart, go to Robbie, please. Don't worry your *keppy.*" She kissed Sara on her forehead. "You shouldn't have to hear these things. Promise me you'll put them out of your mind."

The tumult in Sara's head increased. *Do I have a good father or not?* She couldn't decide. On one hand, her father didn't act like the storybook father in *Honey Bunch* or the TV daddy on *Father Knows Best.* He didn't read the newspaper in the living room or hold Sara on his lap. He never ate breakfast with her and Robbie because he was a butcher who had to be out on the road by 4 a.m. in order to arrive at the 14th Street Market to buy the best meat for Katz and Block Wholesale and Retail Kosher Meats. And he never ate supper with them because he had deliveries to make in Manhattan to important customers.

On the other hand, her daddy was full of smiles when he drove his family in the Oldsmobile to the Bronx Park Zoo and took photos of Sara and Robbie sitting on ponies. He loved visiting Grandma Hannah and Poppy Mo in Little Neck on the weekends and taking the family to see new houses being built on Long Island. She remembered the day when her father pointed to a neat, green ranch house in Levittown and with wide-open eyes talked about the time someday soon when he'd move the family out of Williamsburg and into the suburbs. *Daddy must be a good father. So why did that woman on the telephone say he was taking that dangerous medicine, and why was Mommy so angry after speaking to her?*

In the living room, Robbie wasn't paying attention to *The Merry Mailman.* He was gliding toy cars and trucks around the edges of the room, wherever the rug didn't cover the wooden floor. "Was Mommy crying?" he asked Sara.

Sara didn't want to lie to him, but she didn't want to upset him either. "I'm not sure, Robbie."

"Is Daddy going to be late again?" Robbie blinked his eyes nervously. "Maybe that's why Ma's upset. He must be stuck in traffic." Saying this, Robbie moved his toy truck behind the leg of the club chair. "See?"

Sara flopped onto the couch in the living room and thought about her mother's annoyance when her father began coming home later and later from Katz and Block, sometimes not until 10 p.m. Her mother complained that he was falling asleep in the living room club chair, dropping still-lit cigarettes on the floor, and spending his nights in the chair instead of in their bedroom. Sara herself had noticed the burns, like armies of caterpillars, crawling on the carpet and on the living room end table. She remembered how a rash, like a cluster of strawberries, spread over his neck and arms.

"Just hives," her father explained to her mother one night, his eyes half-closed, his speech slurred. "I've been...oh, I've been...in the store freezer...too long."

"What's wrong with Daddy?" Sara had asked her mother then.

"He's been working extra hours, dear, because he's losing customers. All the small kosher butchers are struggling. Don't worry, darling; he'll be OK."

But Helen wasn't as understanding one Saturday morning a few weeks later when Josef told her he needed to work on Saturdays, too. They stood in the kitchen while Sara sat at the table. "What do you mean?" Helen said. "Your children won't ever see you if you work on Saturdays."

Josef's cheeks turned red. "I can't keep borrowing from Mom and Pop to feed the kids. Besides, the other kosher wholesalers are operating on Saturday. Only the Orthodox shops stay closed."

"Sara," her mother had said, "please go to your room. I need to talk to Daddy."

Even as Sara walked away, she remembered, her mother's voice got louder and louder.

On the living room floor, Robbie was now barricading his truck with blocks under the club chair. Sara wondered how he felt about their father being away so much. "Do you think we have a good daddy, Robbie?"

"A good daddy would be like Superman," he said. "His truck could bust out of jams, *kaboom*!" He pushed all the blocks away from the chair and pulled out the toy truck. "A good daddy could fly like Superman." He lifted the truck in the air, making a high arc, and landed it on the top of the TV, where Rin Tin Tin was barking at some thieves running out of a bank. Robbie's fantasy wasn't what Sara expected. But she heard in his words an echo of what she wished for also.

Sara entered her mother's bedroom to see if she was awake. The air was stale from the odor of cigarettes. "Mommy, I'm hungry," Sara whispered as Helen lay in bed, her eyes half open. Helen raised her body up against the headboard. "Come close, darling, so I can kiss your beautiful cheek. Take apples for yourself and Robbie. I'll make supper soon." She inched herself off the bed. "There's a bottle for Rachel sitting in the saucepan on the stove. If you start feeding her, I'll take over in a few minutes."

Sara was perplexed. Her mother had never asked her to feed Rachel before. Was her mother preparing her for some new responsibilities?

When her father returned home, Sara was already in bed. The bedroom she shared with Robbie was just down the hall from the kitchen, and she could hear her mom begin speaking.

"So you're home early tonight?" Helen's voice, louder than usual, echoed in the quiet apartment.

"I'm tired, Helen," Sara heard her father groan. She strained to hear the rest of his words.

"Bad news," he mumbled. "Manhattan...deliveries..."

"So you have to go out again *tonight*?" The tense ring of her mother's question frightened Sara.

"Yeah," he said. There was a pause. "Thought I'd grab a bite first. What's wrong, Helen? Have you been crying?"

For a moment her mother didn't answer, and then Sara heard her say in an angry voice, "You promised me you'd stay clean!"

Sara didn't know what her mother meant. Was her father dirty?

"What are you talking about?" he said.

"You know what I mean. Mitzi told me the truth."

"Mitzi! You heard from Mitzi? What did she say?"

"The truth, I tell you! The rotten truth."

"The bitch!"

Someone started banging on the table. *It must be Daddy*, Sara thought. The rustle of maple leaves against her bedroom window began to shut out her parents' voices. She just had to hear more clearly what was going on. She rose from her bed, tiptoed barefooted past Robbie, who was still asleep, and closed the door behind her. She slunk down the foyer hallway toward the kitchen and found the swinging door closed. No wonder she had such a hard time hearing their talk. She pushed the door carefully so that it opened just a bit. She saw Josef, his back to her, hovering over Helen near the refrigerator, his arm raised. Then opening the door a little more, standing in the doorway, and rubbing her eyes, she cried, "What's wrong, Mommy?"

Her father swung around in Sara's direction, then quickly turned his back on her. Sara began whimpering. Her mother rushed to embrace her and calm her down. She coaxed Sara back to her bedroom. "*Shush*, honey, everything's OK. Mommy's OK. Daddy and I are just talking."

"So loud!" Sara noticed her mother's swollen eyes.

"We'll keep our voices down, OK? Go back to bed now."

Sara didn't believe that her parents were only talking. She crept out of her bedroom again and quietly made her way to the closed kitchen door where she strained to hear what was happening. Sara pushed the door open a trifle and saw her father crumple into a chair like a balloon losing its air.

"The pressure just kept building up," he complained. He didn't look at Helen as he spoke. He was clasping and unclasping his hands on the kitchen table, large butcher hands with butcher fingers, chunky, calloused, bruised.

"What pressure are you talking about?"

"Pop's pressure. He didn't trust me to be in business by myself. Instead he pushed Irv on me as a partner. That sissy couldn't cut meat!"

Why was her father calling Uncle Irv a sissy?

"That was fifteen years ago!"

"It was supposed to be *my* business—don't you understand?"

Sara saw her father bury his head on the table.

"Look at me!" Helen demanded. "Don't give me these stories, these *bubbe meises*. Your father thought Irv could share the burdens of a new business with you. Have you forgotten that?"

Josef stood up and began nervously marching in place.

Sara was confused. She thought Daddy loved Poppy. She thought Daddy and Uncle Irv were friends.

"You could have disagreed with your father, made another proposal. Why bring up such excuses?"

Shifting from foot to foot, breathing heavily, he stuttered, "N-n-no time. Too much on my mind then. The war...getting married...torn up..."

"Why are you shuffling like that? Stop it. What's wrong with you? Millions of men had to go to war, and they didn't take drugs and wreck their lives like you did."

"But I couldn't handle it!" he shouted. "There you have it." With his arm, he wiped perspiration off his brow.

"*Shush*, not so loud," Helen said, placing a finger on her lips. She shot a glance at the doorway. Sara quickly pulled the door shut.

"You have no idea what I have to deal with, do you?" Sara heard her father yell. "We lost the Front Stage Deli today. The Front Stage! Our biggest account. Did you hear me?" He stormed out of the kitchen and into the living room. Sara ran into the kitchen, where her mother was looking out the window, folding and unfolding her arms and talking to herself.

"May she rest in peace," Helen muttered. "I should have listened to my mother. Stupid, stupid me. She warned me about Josef."

"You're not stupid, Mommy."

"What, *mamela*? You're still up?" Helen turned around. Sara ran to her mother, clung to her sweater, and wouldn't let go.

"Sara, sweetheart, you shouldn't be hearing any of this. I want you to cover your ears. Don't listen! Can you give me your word?" She reached into the broom closet for a tin can that held the rent money and placed a roll of bills into her apron pocket.

Her father came back into the kitchen, ignoring everything in his path, and toppled a chair. "I can stop whenever I want. Whenever I want!"

Sara raced out of the room and hid behind the door again.

"You're a junkie!" Helen hollered, and burst into tears.

"Helen, don't you understand? I'm lost without it. Lost."

"You're lost *with* it!" Helen yelled back. She paused. "Your parents need to know what's happened to their ideal son, their perfect Josef! They need to know what I go through."

"If you dare say a word, you know what I'll do to you!" There was pounding on the table, then complete silence. The only sound was the hum of the refrigerator. Was her mother OK? Sara opened the kitchen door a notch, peeked in, and saw her father shaking his finger accusingly. "Don't you involve my mother, do you hear?"

"I must. This problem is too big for me. I can't handle it on my own."

"No! My mother's had enough trouble." He slammed his fist on the counter. "I'm warning you." His cheeks looked red-hot. "She's never recovered from losing Alex."

"Thank God you feel guilty. You should feel guilty. Maybe your mother can talk sense into you. Me...you're only giving excuses...excuses."

Who was Alex? Sara wondered. Her father was now on his knees. He took her mother's hands. "I'll quit right now. I promise. I'll stop. You'll see. We'll scrape by. Just don't tell my mother."

"Don't be crazy, Josef. Stand up!" she said, pulling her hands away from his. "You need help."

He waved his arms wildly. "No one—*no one*—forces Josef Katz to do anything. Not you. Not my mother. I'll stop when *I'm* good and ready."

"What will happen to us if you get arrested or if you get sick? Don't you think of that?"

"I don't have time to argue with you, Helen. Right now, I need money." He was hopping from one foot to the other, as if he were jumping rope.

"You need money? Where do you expect me to get it from?"

"The rent money."

"Are you out of your mind? We owe your parents that money. You want to make it harder on them?" Her face turned as white as a sheet.

"Just give me the money!"

"I'm not going to feed your habit!" Helen shouted. And when she didn't go to the broom closet to get the money, when Josef saw her back away from him and quickly place her hand in her apron pocket, he lunged at her.

"You're insane!" she screamed, taking hold of the roll of bills and drawing both arms behind her back.

Her father darted toward her like a ferocious King Kong. Sara had seen the monster movie several times on TV and had nightmares about a large ape terrorizing people.

"No! No! Daddy, stop!" Sara saw her father shove her mother against the wall, twist her arm, and rip her apron. Helen seemed defenseless, reminding Sara of the frightened woman King Kong drew into his clutches on top of the Empire State Building. "Daddy, leave her alone! You're hurting Mommy." The small kitchen filled with Sara's shouts and Helen's screams. *It'll be a miracle,* Sara thought, *if this racket doesn't wake Robbie and Rachel up. Maybe they are awake and as frightened as I am.*

Sara suddenly hated her father. She wanted to rush out and topple the gorilla, sweep her mother into her arms, and carry her away to safety. But her legs felt like tree trunks. She watched her mother fall to her knees helplessly. Then King Kong landed a blow on her mother's shoulder, then on her face, forcing her to the floor, causing the bills in her hand to scatter over the linoleum. Sara burst into tears. "Stop it. Stop it, Daddy!"

Her father looked like a crazy person crawling on the floor collecting dollar bills. His movements reminded her of a bum she once saw rummaging through the garbage bin. Josef locked lunatic eyes on Sara and stumbled out of the apartment.

Sara ran to her mother in the kitchen and hugged her. She saw blood dripping from her mother's nose and mouth and an ugly bruise forming on her chin. "Ma, you're hurt!"

"Don't worry, Sara," Helen said, getting up, grabbing a tissue from her pocket. She blotted her bruises and tried putting her disheveled hair in place.

"But Ma, Daddy hit you!"

"He's sick, Sara. He's your father. He didn't deliberately mean to hurt me." She drew Sara close to her and stroked her head.

Sara couldn't understand how her mother could be so kind. *Didn't Daddy just hit and hurt her? Can this monster be my Daddy, the same Daddy who buys us tutti-frutti ice cream cones and takes us to visit Grandma and Poppy?*

"We need to help Daddy," her mother said. "Will you help me? Everything will be fine, dear. Go back to bed, honey. It's our secret, OK?"

As she lay in bed, Sara's thoughts were as chaotic as the tangled maple branches outside her bedroom window. *Does my daddy turn into a wild animal? Does he stalk and prowl at night when there's a full moon like those werewolves in scary movies?*

Fear, mingled with hate, welled up inside her. Her mother was in danger, and she must save her. But how? Sara clenched her teeth. She pictured the sharp, gleaming knife that her father kept in the kitchen drawer, the one he used to carve roast beef and turkey. *Just wait until Daddy comes home.* She lay awake imagining the grainy feel of the knife's wooden handle in her palm. But then she thought: *Do I really want to kill my father?* The father she knew and loved might turn around and say in his jolly voice, "Sara, my Sha-Sha," and she'd feel ashamed. Flooded by feelings of love, fear, and hate, she fell asleep, exhausted.

That night she dreamt that her father met her and Robbie at school. Smiling broadly, he took them for a stroll along the promenade that overlooked the East River and the Brooklyn-Queens Expressway. The sun was shining, the river sparkled.

A strange, masked man appeared just where a set of stone steps led down a steep decline to the expressway. The stranger pulled off his mask. His face was the spitting image of her father's! Totally confused, frightened, she grabbed hold of Robbie.

"I'm your real father," the imposter said, shooting his hand up like a police officer stopping traffic. "You kids have to come with me."

"N-n-no!" the original Josef stammered and stuttered. "Get lost, you f-f-fake!"

Then the bully imposter struck him, and the two of them came to blows. Filled with dread, Sara wanted to root for her stuttering father, but which one of them *was* her real father? She couldn't tell them apart. One father pushed the other down the steps, out of sight. Was he dead? Sara's heart was beating rapidly. Which father was with her now?

Chapter Two

Josef stomped out of the apartment on Sunday morning, headed for his father's butcher shop on Bedford Avenue a few blocks away.

"Keep your mouth closed, Helen, when my mother gets here," he warned. "The little argument we had is no one's business." He grabbed his cap, pulled up his jacket collar, and slid his ledger under his arm. "Pop, Irv, and me, we've got the Front Stage Deli to worry about. So I don't need more trouble from you. You got that?"

Sara stood wobbly-kneed in front of her mother, whose bruises, inflicted by her father a few nights before, were still visible, though Helen had tried to hide them. Sara had watched as her mother carefully put on her lipstick and dabbed makeup on her nose and over the black-and-blue patch on her chin.

Helen didn't contradict Josef. But Sara wondered whether her mother would tell her grandmother about the fight. *How could Ma forget Daddy exploding like a firecracker? How could she ignore his shoving her to the floor when she tried stopping him from taking the rent money?* It was still terrifyingly vivid in Sara's mind.

"Are you going to tell Grandma?" she asked, looking up and staring at the blue-black spot spreading on her mother's chin, beginning to sprout into reds and yellows.

"Sara, sweetheart, let me handle it," her mother said nervously. "This is grown-up stuff. No concern for an eight-year-old. Don't you say anything about it, OK? Just enjoy Grandma's visit." Helen untied the candy-stripe string on the box from Garfield's Bakery and took out the poppyseed cake she had bought for her mother-in-law's visit. She looked at Sara and said, "Grandma's bringing you the Honey Bunch book you wanted."

"Good morning, Helen!" Grandma Hannah barreled into the kitchen. "Your door was open." She set two shopping bags on the table, one filled with freshly plucked chickens, chopped meat, and *kishka* for Helen, the other with colorful rattles and bathtub toys for Rachel, and Paradise Plum suckers, Mickey Mouse Golden Books, and the Honey Bunch book for Sara and Robbie.

"Grandma!" Sara squealed with delight, as she ran up to her and hugged her. She could smell the faint aroma of cinnamon and raisins on her hands.

"Have a seat, Ma," Helen said, just as though everything were normal. "I'll take your coat. A cup of tea?"

"Yes, a cup of tea." Hannah rolled her tongue over her lips. "Do you have any of those *rugelach* left that I brought you last week?"

"I'm sorry, Ma—Josef and the kids ate them all soon after you left."

"They love my baking..."

"Did you bring any chocolate cake for us, Grandma?" Sara asked.

"Not this time, honey. Your grandma's been too busy baking *babka* for the customers. Come, open your book."

"I have a ring cake," Helen said.

"You didn't bake it?"

"You know I don't bake, Ma. My mother never had time to teach me." Helen turned her head toward the window, a faraway look in her eyes. "The poor woman worked six days a week dipping chocolates on an assembly line."

Hannah embraced Helen. "I've shown you how to bake many times."

"I can't concentrate with the baby." Helen started to comb her dark hair with her fingers.

"Okay, a *glasela* tea, some ring cake."

Sara rubbed the sleep out of her eyes. She had not slept soundly since the night of her parents' blow-up. The recurring nightmare about having two fathers kept her awake. Whether her father was pushing her on a swing in Prospect Park, buying her an ice cream cone at the Bronx Zoo, or watching her roller skate on Penn Street, at some point he'd suddenly rip a mask off his face, and a scary man who looked just like him would laugh at her and snarl, "Daddy's here now." Then her father would turn into a hairy King Kong.

Sara yawned and tried to smile as she sat next to her grandmother at the kitchen table. She turned to the first page of her new book.

"Come closer, darling," Hannah said sweetly to Sara, sliding Sara's chair toward her. "Do you have a kiss for Grandma?"

Sara planted a kiss on her grandmother's cheek. She loved her grandmother. She remembered the night Robbie was born, when she was crying for her parents in her grandmother's kitchen. Her father had left for St. Catherine's Hospital to be with her mother all night, while he waited for Sara's new baby brother.

"You want Grandma should show you the secret of my chocolate cake?" she had asked Sara then. She dropped spoons full of the secret ingredients onto Sara's tongue. The syrupy mixture of sugar and melted dark chocolate, along with the pleasant sting of rum, were enough to dissolve Sara's feelings of abandonment.

Grandma could fix all ills, Sara thought. *She would surely know how to help Daddy when she learns about his problem.*

Helen returned to the kitchen cradling the whining Rachel at her left hip. Sara watched her mother lift the teapot with her right hand. She seemed like a magician or a juggler to Sara, as she poured one cup of tea, then another, at the same time that she rocked the crying baby back to sleep.

"My children used to nap in the morning," Hannah said. "But they didn't wake up cranky, because I gave them milk or juice before they fell asleep."

"Good idea," Helen said calmly. Rachel continued crying.

"Sheyna maidel," Hannah said, pinching Sara's cheek. Sara nestled into her grandmother's lap, enjoying the comfort of her broad thighs.

"Why so serious, little one?" Hannah asked. "Is something bothering you?"

"Sara's just tired, Ma," Helen answered.

"Sleepy girl," Hannah said. "Apple of your Daddy's eye. He'd do anything for you."

Sara rested her head on her grandmother's chest.

"Sara," Helen whispered, "Rachel is finally dozing. I'd like to put her back in her crib. Can you please bring Grandma the cake I put on the tray? And when you finish eating your piece of cake, I want you to mind your sister."

"Where is Robbie?" Grandma Hannah asked Sara.

"He's at his friend's house, across the street," Sara replied, pointing out the window at Penn Street, already crowded with people strolling and cars honking.

"Such traffic," Hannah remarked as Helen returned to the kitchen, a cigarette in her lips. Hannah looked on disapprovingly when Helen lit the cigarette. "The boy could get hurt in all that traffic."

Helen looked directly at her mother-in-law. "You needn't worry. I know how to care for my children."

"Forgive me," Hannah apologized. "I say the wrong things. I know you're a good mother. You're also a lucky mother." She sneezed, took out a handkerchief, and blew her nose. She pointed to a photo of Josef at the zoo with the children on the shelf above the kitchen desk. "Look how he adores his kids."

"But the truth is, *I'm* the one keeping this family together," Helen blurted out, motioning for Sara to stand next to her.

"What?" Hannah grunted. "You leave Josef out? How come? He works night and day for you and the kids. He's always thinking about his family. He just asked Pop and me for money to tide you and the kids over…until he and Irv make up the losses from the Front Stage Deli."

"What?" Helen's lips pursed. "Josef promised me he wasn't going to borrow any more money from you and Pop."

"You need to live, don't you?" Hannah said, raising an eyebrow.

"You have no idea what your son is up to," Helen said. "I can't say any more in front of Sara." She hugged Sara tightly.

"Yes, you can, Ma," Sara piped up.

"Sara, I want you to be quiet and watch Rachel while I speak to Grandma. Go in the bedroom and don't wake up your sister. You can take the storybook Grandma brought for you to read." Helen took Sara's hand and ushered her out of the kitchen. But Sara turned around and stood in the kitchen doorway, where she could see and hear her mother and grandmother. She noticed her mother tapping her fists on the table.

"What are you so tense about, Helen?" Hannah asked, staring at Helen's white knuckles.

"Am I tense?" Helen stopped tapping. The kitchen clock ticked. "Your son...the good father... I hate to tell you this.... I'm sick over it. Josef's using hard drugs, Ma. Heroin. He's addicted."

"What are you talking about, *addicted?* Why would you make up such a vicious story? I can't believe you'd do that."

"It's no story, Ma. I've been living with this for days. The money Josef borrowed from you and Pop—it's gone. He used it to buy drugs. I'm beside myself. I don't know what to do." Helen said, her voice breaking.

Hannah paced back and forth in the kitchen. "How do you *know* for sure that Josef's taking...what...'heroin'?"

"Mitzi, Spencer's wife, told me. Spencer and Josef are in it together."

"Spencer is a liar," Grandma snapped.

"No, it's the truth. Josef admits it. He pleaded with me not to tell you, but I feel I have no choice. Nothing I say to him makes any difference. He says he wants to stop, but he can't control himself. Poor Sara! On top of everything, the child knows all about it. It just breaks my heart."

Sara listened with wide eyes from the doorway. She heard her grandmother mumble something in Yiddish, but she wasn't able to make the words out. Hannah dropped into a chair and moaned.

"Without heroin, Ma, he acts like a madman. He's already turned on me." Helen pointed to her chin with its ugly bruise.

Hannah gasped. "My Josef did that?"

Helen nodded. "I'm afraid, Ma, that he might harm the kids…or himself," Helen cried, folding her arms around herself. "For the children's sake, we have to do something."

Hannah wailed, "It can't be true. Oh, my God!" She looked around the room. "I wish it was another woman! Not this shame, this *umglick*."

"Why…why do you wish that, for God's sake?" Helen's voice cracked. "How do you think…that makes *me* feel?"

"At least we'd know what to do," Hannah said, rising from the chair and adjusting her dress. "We'd talk him out of it, get rid of her. It's a more *normal* problem."

Helen stared at her mother-in-law. "You think infidelity is less serious than addiction? Maybe skirt chasers have worse character defects than addicts."

"My Josef has no defects in his character."

What's infidelity? Sara wondered. Another word she'd never heard before.

"Sit down, Ma. Listen. With the drugs inside him, he seems to manage. He's cheerful. You can see for yourself. He's Mr. Personality with the Manhattan deli owners. But without the drugs, he's Mr. Hyde. That's the person I see. He's hooked, plain and simple. We need to find him medical help—a good doctor to wean him off heroin."

Hannah waved her hand at Helen. "*You're* the devil infecting him. I know the truth. I've known all along. I know what you did in the clubrooms before you got married." She shook her head back and forth, clucking her tongue. "What a shame, what a *shandah*."

"What's wrong with you?" Helen shouted. "It's your son who has the problem, not me. He dragged me to those clubrooms. Don't you remember? You knew he had a problem and you wanted him to shape up. So you had him marry me. But he was already hooked, Ma. Something is missing in him. Drugs agree with him."

"Something is missing?" Hannah took deep breaths. "Yes, that's it," she said knitting her brows. "Maybe he's missing something...when you two...you know...come together. Tell me, Helen, how do you two have sex?"

"Huh? What are you talking about?"

Hannah put her hand to her mouth and whispered, but Sara could still hear, "Maybe you're just not *satisfying* my Josef." Her eyes flashed with a strange fire. "Maybe you need to let him *shtoop* you, from the rear."

"Is that how *you* do it with Poppy?" Helen screamed, moving away from her. "You get out of here right now." She raised her arm and pointed to the door. "What nerve! I eat my heart out over your son, and you try to blame me—and shame me with your insults. Get out! Get out!"

Sara never heard such frightening words pass between her mother and grandmother. *Why are Grandma and Ma so angry? Doesn't Grandma want to help Daddy fix his problem?*

Hannah started to rise, but then she fell back down into the chair, her eyes rolling as if she were going to faint. Helen ran for tissues, wiped Hannah's forehead, helped her to sit up, and encouraged her to sip from a glass of water. Slowly she regained her composure.

"Are you OK, Grandma?" Sara called out, forgetting that she wasn't supposed to be there.

Hannah caught a glimpse of Sara in the doorway, but she didn't answer. Instead, she pushed Helen's hands away and stood up. "What a migraine," she cried, holding her head. "Oh, how can I live? I'm going to die." She walked toward Sara, who was now in the room. "Sara, sweetheart, you've heard what we've been saying. Oh, I wish you hadn't. Come to me, darling." Again, she pinched Sara's cheek and called her *sheyna meidel.* "Darling, it's up to you," she whispered in Sara's ear. "You know how proud your father is of you. You need to speak to your Daddy, Sara. You've got to tell him he must stop ruining his family."

"Me, Grandma?"

Hannah put her arms around Sara. "Your father will listen to you. He would never want to hurt his little girl."

"What are you telling her?" Helen exclaimed. "Leave her alone. She shouldn't be hearing this. It's not fit for a child."

Turmoil filled Sara's mind. How could *she* possibly talk to her father about his problem? He'd already turned into a monster, a gorilla, in her mind. She'd wanted to slice him up with his roast beef knife. But, then, she didn't really want to hurt him. By the same token, she didn't want *him* harming anyone in her family, either. *Does Grandma know that if I talk to my father, I won't know which father I'll be talking to? Does she know about the masked man? And if I speak to the wrong father, does she know he could push and shove and hurt me like he hurt Ma a few nights ago, when he turned into King Kong in the kitchen? Will King Kong even talk to a little girl?*

Feeling smaller by the second, Sara ran out of the room, waving goodbye and saying, "I've got homework to do!" She retreated into the safety of her parents' bedroom and shut the door behind her. She stepped in front of the mirror on her mother's dressing table and saw Rachel behind her, sleeping soundly in the crib. Her grandmother's words repeated in her mind, "Your father will listen to you. He would never want to hurt his little girl." *Yes, someone has to stop Daddy from ruining the family. Should it be me? Lately Daddy's been ignoring me. Would he even listen to me?*

She imagined herself speaking to her father in whispers, as he sat sleeping in the living room club chair. "Daddy," she'd say, pretending to see him there in the mirror. She would tap his hand and awaken him.

"What is it, Sara?" He'd raise one eyelid at a time.

"Daddy," she would stammer and tremble.

"Don't play games with me, Sara." Daddy would tighten his lips and broaden his nostrils.

"Daddy, I want..."

"Want what?" he'd shout, standing up and towering above her.

She would try to form the words. "Daddy, you scare us. You hurt Mommy even though she loves you. We have to hide your problem, but we know you have one. Why can't you get better and spend more time with us?"

But Sara was afraid that when she actually faced her father in real life, she wouldn't find the right words. Maybe no words at all would come out of her mouth. She looked in the mirror again and saw the tears running down her cheeks. She wished Grandma Hannah hadn't asked her to talk to her father. It was too hard.

Chapter Three | 1956

A drab gray Saturday morning followed a December snowfall.

"It's him!" Sara said, taking Robbie's hand. They had begged their mother all morning to let them watch for their father from the fire escape outside their bedroom window. Helen finally allowed them to sit outside, after they promised not to stand anywhere near the edge. The fire escape was usually reserved for hot, summer nights, but this winter morning was an exception. Their father was returning home after a six-month stay at a hospital in Lexington, Kentucky.

Bundled up in woolen jackets and scarves, they watched cars and trucks pass by on Penn Street, splashing up slush until finally the sixth checkered cab they counted stopped where they lived. Their father's felt fedora peeked out of the taxi. Sara restrained herself from shouting "Daddy"— after all, she wasn't sure which father would be returning home: her real father or the imposter-father of her nightmares, the one Grandma Hannah told her to chase away.

Sara remembered that dreadful morning last year when her mother revealed her father's drug addiction to her grandmother for the first time. Sara remembered how Grandma Hannah had told her to talk to her father—that he would listen to her. That she could be the one to save their family.

Sara felt guilty for not speaking up to her father before he left for Lexington. She just couldn't do it. He hadn't wanted to go to the hospital, but her mother and grandmother persuaded him, and reluctantly he went. Sara worried whether his stay at Lexington had been successful or not. He received a treatment there her mother called by the strange name "cold turkey."

When Sara had asked her mother what "cold turkey" meant, Helen said she didn't really know, but she guessed the treatment would cause her father to feel the chills. Sara wondered if her mother was being completely honest. *Did Ma know more about cold turkey than she was willing to say?* Seeing her father now on the wintry street, Sara thought of the unlucky turkey she and Robbie had recently cried over on the TV show *I Remember Mama*. The Hansen children on the show loved a turkey that lived in the barn behind their house. Affectionately they named him Tom and visited him each evening after the weather turned cold. When Thanksgiving came, six-year-old Robbie asked his nine-year-old sister why the Hansen children had trouble eating the turkey that sat stuffed on their holiday table. And when Sara explained that the turkey that had lived in their barn sadly was now on their table, Robbie had frowned and said, teary-eyed, "But the Hansen children *loved* Tom."

Sara wondered if "cold turkey" meant that one of her fathers had to be killed. Had the scary shadow-father been killed—or was it the father she and Robbie loved? She had to admit, even after all her guesses about cold turkey, she was still confused. She led her brother back into the apartment and shouted to her mother, "Daddy's home!"

Helen was in the kitchen watching one-year-old Rachel feed herself Cheerios from the tray of her high chair. "Daddy will be so happy to see you children, but he'll be tired and hungry. So don't ask him too many questions, OK?"

"May I show him my new Toni doll?" Sara asked.

"Can I show him my erector set?" Robbie piped up.

"Yes, sweethearts. But not right away."

Sara and Robbie said in unison, "We love you, Daddy!" when their father entered the apartment, dropped his suitcase, crouched down, and opened his arms to embrace them. He looked up at Helen without speaking.

Still embracing the children, he finally said, "I missed you kids."

"Let's have Mommy's special brunch," Sara said, hoping that the father who'd be eating lox and eggs with them would be her loving father, not the sick, angry man who went away. Her loving father nicknamed her Sha-sha and whisked her to safety one summer when she broke her arm. Her loving father visited her public school once on Parents' Night and, because she and Robbie did well in school, promised to take them to Radio City Music Hall to see the Rockettes. Would the father hugging them now remember his promise? Would he play the harmonica the way he used to?

Sara suspected that this slimmer man whose cheeks looked hollow and who left potatoes on his plate was not her real Daddy. Her real Daddy always ate everything on his plate.

"Will you play your harmonica for us, Daddy?" she asked, with a slight tremble in her voice.

Josef's eyes looked vacant.

"Sara," Helen said, "give Daddy time. Let him relax a bit. Don't be so impatient."

To Sara this meant that Daddy still had his problem. If she wanted him to get better, she'd have to do what was harder than anything else she'd ever imagined. She would have to talk to him about his addiction, just as Grandma had asked.

Later that night, when Sara's parents were in the kitchen, their voices loud and shrill, Sara was afraid to fall asleep, afraid the imposter-father would turn up again in her dreams.

Sara overslept Sunday morning. She and Robbie were supposed to accompany their father to Little Neck to visit their grandparents. But there was no sign of Robbie. *Did Daddy already leave without me?*

Still groggy, Sara heard muffled sounds coming from the kitchen. At first she thought they were Rachel's. But no—it was her mom talking on the telephone. Minutes later, fully awake, and straining to hear, Sara could make out her mother's sad words.

"He never expected to leave Lexington alive."

Who is Ma talking to? What happened in Lexington? Is Daddy cured? Is there still time for me to talk with Daddy?

Sara tiptoed quietly into her parents' bedroom and carefully lifted the receiver from the extension phone. She crossed her fingers, hoping the click hadn't been too loud.

"He told me cold turkey is like dying. And the answer to your question is no. He's not cured."

"You mean the doctors couldn't help him?"

"Oh, Annette," her mother cried, "he said those doctors are heartless. He said his body ached all over with muscle cramps and chills. Just the touch of water made him feel like he was burning up. And he constantly had a sickening taste in his mouth. But he said the doctors did nothing, as if they were punishing him, like a criminal or a...a...sinner." Then her voice dropped. "He told me...some men...had heart attacks and strokes...and were left to die."

Sara almost cried out loud. *Daddy could have died!* But she kept quiet and tried not to breathe too heavily into the receiver.

"You believe what he tells you about the doctors?"

"I do, Annette. I do. Because he's told me the truth about everything else."

"Everything else?"

"About how he was able to survive."

"God, Helen, how *did* he survive?"

"He managed...to get heroin. That's how."

Sara heard the frustration and sadness in her mother's voice.

"He got that stuff in the hospital?" Annette asked.

Sara felt confused and terrified. *If heroin was making Daddy sick, why did he need it to survive?* Still, she kept silent. Her mother mustn't know she was listening in.

"He told me he bribed someone," her mother sighed. "A person on the staff brought the stuff to him and the others."

"Sounds impossible! What about security?"

"Security?" Her mother's voice rose. "Security can't detect it."

"Why not?"

And then her mother's words became barely audible. Sara tried extra hard to hear. "They...carry...the stuff..."

Her mother paused for a long time, breathing rapidly.

Why is Ma afraid to talk?

"Whoever it was," Helen finally said, "he carried the heroin in his behind."

Sara almost gagged. She covered her mouth with her hand. She couldn't imagine anyone carrying a package of anything in his bottom—and then to think that her father put that stuff into his body! She felt like vomiting, but she held her breath.

"I asked Josef, 'How could the doctors let you get away with smuggling drugs inside? How could they put you through all your pain and suffering for nothing?' And you know what he told me? He said the doctors know cold turkey doesn't work."

"No! That can't be. Why would they use a treatment that doesn't work?"

"He said they're conducting experiments, using the men like guinea pigs!"

"I can't believe it," her aunt exclaimed. "Can you?"

"I don't think he's lying. After all, he admits he's still using drugs. At least he's not deceiving me about that anymore."

Sara was so startled and overwhelmed, she had to put the receiver down. *How terrible! They experimented on Daddy! That's why he's so weak and tired.* She almost belted the word "criminals" out loud. But that would have given her away and angered her mother greatly. She managed to keep still and picked the phone up again as delicately as she could.

"I told Josef he *has* to get off heroin!" she heard her mother cry. "Lexington arranged for him to see a doctor in Manhattan, a psychiatrist. But he said he wouldn't go. He doesn't trust Lexington. Not after what they put him through."

"Does he have an alternative?" Annette asked.

"There's methadone. It's a new treatment. But it only substitutes one habit for another. And there's shock therapy." Her mother began sobbing. "I don't blame Josef for rejecting that."

The more Sara heard, the more alarmed she became. *Shock therapy? Is that like an electric chair? Can't Daddy die from that, too?* Again, she held her breath.

"Helen, what will you do?"

"I insisted that he see the doctor in Manhattan. 'It's not only about you,' I said to him. 'It's about us, your family. We love you and need you to get well. Are you just going to let your body rot from heroin until you drop dead? You need the help of a doctor!'" Her mother sounded beside herself.

Sara could hardly wait for their conversation to end. She was afraid her father was going to die, but she bottled up her fears inside. That day, and for many days afterward, she wasn't able to do her fourth-grade homework for Mrs. Grady. She ate too many Chunky candy bars and broke out in pimples. And she developed headaches and stomach cramps. Her worrying seemed to have no end.

At Helen's insistence, Josef finally agreed to visit Dr. Clayton in Manhattan two evenings a week, appointments he continued for more than a year. Hoping her father would improve, Sara watched to see if these visits would produce any changes. After a few months, she saw her father coming back to life. She was overjoyed and wondered what kind of magic spell Dr. Clayton had cast over him. There must be *some* doctors, she thought, who care about their patients and want to help them.

With an energy Sara hardly thought possible, her father

bounded back to work with Uncle Irv in Katz and Block Kosher Meats. Promptly at three-thirty each weekday morning, he left Penn Street for the meat market on 14th Street. When he arrived home after work, he liked to brag to Sara about how strong he was. He would stand before the bedroom mirror in his work pants and undershirt, looking at himself and flexing his muscles. He'd boast that single-handedly he had hauled the heavy forequarters of several cows onto his van, driven them from the market over the bridge back to Williamsburg, and unloaded them into his butcher shop freezer. "No trouble at all," he'd say, laughing.

On some mornings, Sara was awake early enough to listen to Josef getting ready in the bathroom, the faucets running and lots of clinking and rattling. *What are those sounds? Is Daddy dropping his razor into the sink?* Then she'd hear the click of the bathroom door being locked. A hush would come over the apartment, and Sara would try to go back to sleep.

On the evenings he traveled into Manhattan to see Dr. Clayton, he didn't return home until nine at night. Allowed to stay up an extra hour beyond their usual bedtime, Sara and Robbie were happy to see their father act jolly when he arrived home. He was proud that his old customers, Hymie's Deli and Al's Sixth Avenue, were sticking with him.

"They love my free bonuses of chicken livers and sweet breads," he chuckled. "And they're still thanking me for my oyster steaks. Their customers love them. Kosher filet mignon!"

He was pleased that he was attracting new accounts when, sadly, other kosher butchers were going out of business. On the kitchen table, he'd place brown paper bags filled to the brim with poultry and meat. One by one, he happily unfolded the shiny white butcher-paper packages containing the family suppers for the week: chicken, freshly plucked; deep red chopped meat; slippery brown liver; and *flanken* for stewing. With gusto, he ate the late dinners Helen prepared for him. Then he'd take his harmonica out and serenade the family with show tunes from *Porgy and Bess* and *My Fair Lady.*

Daddy's getting better, Sara thought. *Maybe the scary imposter won't return. Maybe I won't have to talk to him about his problem after all.*

Chapter Four | 1957

When Josef saw Dr. Clayton in Manhattan on weeknights after work, he would drive into Manhattan again on Saturday mornings. He told Helen he was shoring up his bonds with kosher-style delis that were his new customers.

"Dad, do you *have* to go into the city today?" Sara asked on one of those Saturdays. "We'd all like you to stay at home. Besides, Saturdays are so relaxing in our neighborhood, so quiet and peaceful, now that the Orthodox families are observing Sabbath."

He glanced over at Helen, who was busy at the sink washing breakfast dishes. "Lots of Jews like us don't keep the Sabbath strictly," he said. "My customers' delis are filled with people on Saturdays. And they love meeting me, the man who brings them delicacies."

Sara knew her mother's feelings on the matter. "Ma would rather you wouldn't go. Right, Ma?" Helen nodded in agreement.

"But I need the business, ladies."

Helen had told Sara many times she preferred Josef spending weekends with his children at home. "Manhattan is...well, it's dangerous for him," she had told Sara.

"Dangerous, Ma? Come on." To Sara, Manhattan meant Broadway shows, Macy's parades, and Central Park. And now Manhattan also meant Dr. Clayton.

"Forget what I said about danger," her mother replied. "I just wish your father didn't work on Saturdays." She paused. "Maybe I shouldn't be so critical. I know he wants to pay Grandma and Poppy back for Dr. Clayton's fees."

All the talk this morning around "Saturday" piqued Sara's curiosity. "Can you take Robbie and me with you to Manhattan, Daddy? I'm ten, you know."

"And I'm seven, Dad!" Robbie declared, as he drank chocolate milk at the table. Two-year old Rachel was in her playpen, raising her arms and waiting to be lifted up and out.

A smile spread across Josef's face. He was finishing his coffee. "I'd love my customers to meet *my* young lady and *my* young man. Can you two be ready in fifteen minutes?"

Helen was not enthusiastic. "You better think about it first, Josef. Is it really a good idea bringing the kids with you? They could be a distraction. I just don't know."

"Don't be a worrywart. My customers know I'm a family man. The kids should see what their daddy does. C'mon, Helen. We'll be fine."

To the children he added, "On our drive home, we'll pick up those Radio City Music Hall tickets I promised you."

"Oh, Daddy," Robbie giggled. "You remembered."

"Of course, sonny boy." He tousled Robbie's blond hair.

As Sara and Robbie put their hats and coats on, Rachel began to whine. "Want to go with Daddy!"

Josef gave Rachel a kiss. "I'll bring you home a big cookie, sweetheart."

"No! Want to go!"

"Next time, honey," Helen said. "When Mommy goes with

Daddy, Rachel will go, too. Please stay at home with Mommy! Mommy doesn't want to be alone." She gave Rachel a zwieback cracker and sat her in the high chair, then helped Robbie snap the strap of his hat around his neck to protect against the winter chill.

"You be Daddy's navigator," Helen whispered into Sara's ear, as she left the apartment. "OK, honey? Watch out for yourself and your brother."

Josef drove his van over the Williamsburg Bridge—Robbie seated next to him, Sara by the door. Waiting for backed-up traffic on Delancy Street to ease, Josef tapped his fingers on the steering wheel, took his harmonica out of his shirt pocket, and started to play "Yankee Doodle."

"Sing along, kids," he said. Sara and Robbie sang—and they continued singing even after Josef put his harmonica down and drove uptown. Sara couldn't remember her father ever being so cheerful. *What a change,* she thought, *from how he was when he returned from Lexington. Dr. Clayton must be doing a good job. Maybe he's already cured Daddy, and I won't have to tell Daddy that he must get better.*

When the traffic seemed to thin out near Klein's Department Store on Union Square, Josef suddenly began sailing through red lights. Sara became frightened, watching them whiz past storefronts and pedestrians. *Why is Daddy in such a hurry? Why isn't he stopping at red lights?* "Daddy, you're going too fast. Watch the lights!"

Then, abruptly, he stopped at Sam Goody's record store and double-parked in front of the entrance. A crowd was gathering—people were milling about, waving notebooks and flashing cameras.

"Why are we stopping here, Daddy?" Robbie asked.

"Don't you want Johnny Mathis's autograph?" he said, giving him a hug.

"You mean he's *here*?" Sara shouted.

"That's why I stopped, silly! Don't you see the crowds?" He beamed at her. "Trust me, Sha-sha."

Sara liked hearing her father call her "Sha-sha." It made her feel close to him. She and Robbie laughed. Just the week before, they had heard Johnny Mathis sing on *The Ed Sullivan Show.*

"You stay in the van, Sha-sha." He turned the radio on and took Robbie into the record shop. Sara knew it wasn't right for them to be double-parked. As she waited for them to return, she listened to a station playing Jimmie Rodgers' "Honeycomb," and she watched the crowds on the street, hoping no policeman would notice the van and issue a ticket.

The Everly Brothers were singing "Wake Up Little Susie" when Robbie climbed back into the van and shook the signed photo in Sara's face. "What a swell guy!" he said.

Josef continued to drive uptown, ignoring more red lights. When they passed the dome of the planetarium, he cried out, "Hoo-ha! That's where Mr. Hayden does his jamming."

"Slow down, Daddy!" Sara said. "You're scaring me."

"Can we stop at the planetarium, Daddy?" Robbie asked. "We're studying the stars in school."

"Next time, sonny boy," Josef said, speeding on.

They finally parked on the Upper West Side and walked toward Sharkie's Deli, one of Josef's customers. They passed people on Broadway carrying bags and packages emitting wonderful smells: the anise-like fragrance of corn rye with caraway seeds; the thick, vanilla-almond sweetness of *halvah*; and the pickled scent of fresh herring. Josef introduced his children to Mr. Golden, the deli owner, who smiled and shook their hands.

"Come in; sit down a minute," said Mr. Golden, a man with puffy cheeks, a bulbous nose, and red hair. He showed Sara and Robbie to a table and treated them to cream soda, baked apples, and sugar cookies, while Josef went over some paperwork with him at the cash register.

When they were ready to leave, Josef pointed to the display cases. "All from *my* butcher shop," he told Sara and Robbie proudly, "the salami and bologna sausages, the pastrami, the tongue, and the corned beef."

Mr. Golden put his arm around Robbie. "Your daddy's meat is the best in the city. Come back with your mother, young fellow. Have a dinner on the house. How's that?"

Robbie looked up, smiled at Mr. Golden, and shook his head up and down. "Thank you, Mr. Golden. Yes, we will."

On the way home they drove through Central Park and stopped at Radio City to pick up their tickets. Then Josef surprised them again. "Hey, kids! We're almost at Greenwich Village. They've got the best Italian ices in the city."

"Do they have cherry, Daddy?" Robbie asked.

"They even have pistachio!" he said, grinning. He honked his horn as they passed the corner of Second Avenue and Twenty-Third Street. "There's Dr. Clayton's office," he said pointing to a door between two restaurants.

"So that's where you go," Sara said. She thought the office would have looked more dignified.

Sara was fascinated as they drove up Sixth Avenue near Bleecker Street. All the activity on the sidewalks! An outdoor art show, men holding other men's hands, women with their arms around each other and wearing heavy makeup. Josef parked the car, and they walked down Eighth Street.

A tall Negro man with frizzy hair and a crossed eye shouted at Josef as he passed them on the street. A blonde woman wearing rhinestone slippers was holding the Negro's hand. Robbie hid behind his father's legs. "Qué pasa, mi hombre?" the man asked Josef.

"Ats-whay appening-hay? Oo-yay ave-hay uff-stay?" Josef answered, slapping the man's hand. Sara recognized the Spanish, but not her father's words. She thought she saw the man give her father something, but she couldn't quite see what it was before he quickly placed the item in his pocket. As they walked ahead, Sara asked, "Do you know those people, Daddy?"

Josef shook his head. "Not really."

"But you slapped hands together."

"That doesn't mean anything. The people here are just friendly."

"What did you say to him?" Sara asked.

Josef looked up, searching the clouds for his answer. "It was Pig Latin...a greeting."

"What's Pig Latin, Daddy?" Robbie asked.

"It's slang. I'll teach it to you and Sha-sha."

"And what did that guy hand you?" Sara asked.

"Nothing—just some announcement. They pass them out all the time."

"They don't do that in our neighborhood," Sara said. She gazed at the people on the streets: Negroes, Hispanics, and Asians mixing with the whites; men wearing berets and sandals, even in the cold; women in tight black leotards and colorful, flowing scarves, their hair long and loose with square-cut bangs. *The women in our neighborhood wear suits and dresses, and the Orthodox women only wear dark colors and cover their heads with scarves or wigs and their arms with long sleeves. In our neighborhood, I can tell who belongs where just by how they dress.*

"These people seem different," Sara said out loud. "Do they all get along together?"

"Down here," Josef said, speaking slowly and haltingly, "lots of different people mix with one another."

"This is the first time I've seen a Negro man with a white woman," Sara said. She realized that the only Negroes she actually knew were in her fifth-grade class. That was because Negro and Puerto Rican families were just beginning to move into Williamsburg, but they lived on streets set apart from hers. *Wouldn't it be nice*, she thought, *to have a Negro friend*?

"Do you think they're married, Daddy?" Robbie asked.

"I don't know, son," he said slowly, rolling his eyes. "Sometimes people are together just because they like each other."

"What about those other people on the street?" Sara asked. "Like those two men holding hands. Do you know them?"

"They're homosexuals, Sara." Josef paused. "They like to be with people of the same sex. Good people come in all colors and sexes. The important thing is not to judge someone because of what you see on the outside."

"I know that, Dad," Robbie said. "Rabbi Korn tells us that in Hebrew school."

Josef bent down to meet Robbie eye to eye. "It's too bad the rabbi doesn't tell you that Negroes and homosexuals are pushed aside the same way Jewish people are. We're all people...in the same boat. Pretty soon we'll be seeing more integration in our neighborhood."

"What's 'integration'?" Robbie asked.

"Different people mixing, like they do here." He paused again, looked at his children, and tilted his head. "How about those ices I promised?"

"Everything OK?" Sara's mother asked when the three of them arrived home. A warm smile lit up her face. Sara nodded and showed her mother the autographed photo.

"Oh, my!" Helen said. "Johnny Mathis?" She looked at Josef, who was perspiring.

"You went all the way to Sam Goody's? Where do you get your energy?"

"We also passed Dr. Clayton's office," Sara said. "Then we went to Greenwich Village and saw homosexuals and lots of Negroes with white people."

A sober expression replaced Helen's smile. "Why did you take them to the Village, Josef?"

"We got Italian ices, Ma," Robbie interrupted.

"The best in the city!" Josef said with a grin. "You can't keep these kids in a shell forever, Helen."

"Did you ever hear of Pig Latin, Ma?" Sara asked.

"Pig Latin? Yes, your father and I spoke it as teenagers. Do you know it?"

"Es-yay," Sara said smiling. "Daddy taught us."

"That's nice," Helen said, eyeing Josef with suspicion. "I see your father was very busy with you two today. Maybe, if Daddy's not too tired, he can practice Pig Latin with you while I go out for a short spell. Annette would like me to take the bus with her to downtown Brooklyn. I'll leave Rachel with you. Is that OK, Josef?"

"That's fine, Helen," Josef said. "You go—I've got things under control."

Helen gazed at him again. "Are you sure?"

"Sure," he said, and he stepped lightly toward the credenza in the living room as if he were floating. In the living room, he went over to a set of Lionel trains he had mounted on a large sheet of plywood for Robbie a few weeks ago. "C'mon, sonny boy," he called to Robbie. "Let's get these trains started."

After her mother left, the scene in the living room filled Sara with feelings of affection for her family. Rachel lay on the rug watching cartoons on television, eating a sugar cookie her father had brought her. Robbie conducted his trains. Josef relaxed in his club chair, browsing through *Butcher Workmen* magazines piled on his lap. Sara was happy to see her father spending time at home, taking time to read. She was also happy to know what a good teacher he was. What he said that morning about accepting different kinds of people was just what she was learning in Mrs. Martin's class. She couldn't wait to recite a poem for him that she had memorized for her school declamation contest: "The Little Black Boy" by William Blake. While the others were occupied, Sara stepped into her parents' bedroom, stood before their large bureau mirror, and began rehearsing so she could impress her father:

My mother bore me in the southern wile,
And I am black,
But O, my soul is white.
White as an angel is the English child,
But I am black,
As if bereaved of light...

How pleased Daddy will be. I'd much rather recite this poem to him than talk to him about how he needs to stay cured and healthy. Yet she wondered if she was avoiding something important. Her failure to approach him about his condition began troubling her, but she tried putting it out of her mind.

She returned to the living room, eager to recite the poem. She saw her father getting up from the club chair with difficulty, the magazines on his lap dropping to the floor. As he bent down to gather them, his arms twitched as if they were thick, quivering rubber bands. Clumsily he got to his feet and rushed to the bathroom. Sara was alarmed, and she wasn't sure how to respond.

Meanwhile Rachel cried, "Where Daddy go? Daddy. Daaad-dy!" When her father didn't answer, she wailed, "When Mommy coming home?" She ran in her father's direction. Because Josef hadn't shut the bathroom door completely, when Rachel reached for the knob, the door opened, and she toppled into the room.

"Rachel, stop!" Sara shouted.

"Get out! You don't belong in here," Josef hollered. "Shoo! Shoo! Move!"

Sobbing loudly, Rachel ran from the bathroom into her parents' bedroom and dove onto their bed.

Daddy didn't have to get so angry at Rachel, Sara thought. She heard her father in the bathroom, the faucet drip-drip-dripping, glass and metal sounds clanking in the sink. She trembled, recognizing those sounds—her father's early-morning bathroom sounds—and now she suspected those sounds were a bad sign.

"What happened?" Sara asked when her father emerged from the bathroom, fastening his belt. Sara smelled something pungent and burning, an odor that sometimes lingered in the bathroom after her father came out. She remembered her recurring nightmare of her father's scary double. *What if Daddy's being controlled again by the monster?*

"You keep out of it, kid!" her father growled at her, his eyes narrowing.

Yes, her father even looked different now. Something terrible had definitely taken hold of him. *But how was that possible? Wasn't he seeing Dr. Clayton? Is it because of me, because I broke my promise to Grandma? Is it my fault?*

Then suddenly, as if nothing at all were wrong, Josef began speaking softly. "Kids, no problem! No problem at all." He walked into his bedroom, swooped Rachel up in his beefy arms and crooned, "Don'tcha know, sweetie pie, you have to knock before you come into a bathroom— knocka, knocka!" He took his harmonica out of his pocket and began blowing the familiar sounds of "Yankee Doodle." Rachel sucked her thumb and calmed down enough to return to the living room.

"How about milkshakes, kids?" Josef asked as he walked unsteadily into the kitchen. "We have tutti frutti ice cream." He laughed loudly.

Sara nervously watched her father from the kitchen doorway. He was pouring milk into the blender and spilling much of it onto the linoleum floor. She watched him add ice cream, splashing milk onto the counter in the process. She saw how he nearly slipped on the puddles he was making. Slowly, he poured the foamy pink liquid into four large glasses and carried them on a tray into the living room.

Exactly how it happened Sara couldn't explain, but Josef somehow tripped on the threshold of the kitchen door, lost his balance, and knocked the swinging door loose. The door landed right smack on his left hand as he carried the tray, and like a sideways slicing machine, the door cut his chunky middle finger in two.

"Aieee!" he screamed, as the glasses, the tray, and the milk flew across the foyer, along with the tip of his middle finger. He grimaced in pain. He took quick short breaths and moaned. The children had never heard their father cry out like that before. Blood gushed from his hand.

"Call an ambulance," Sara yelled hysterically, forgetting that she was the one who should be making the call. But she couldn't move; her feet were riveted to the floor.

It was Robbie who ran to the phone and dialed the operator. "Help us pleeease! We're on Penn Street, number 1673, apartment 2B. My daddy chopped his finger off. Send an ambulance—please hurry!"

Sara wished she could hide until she figured out what to do. Finally she was able to bring Josef a large white towel from the bathroom. He wrapped the towel around his hand. Blood spread through the cloth in red zigzags.

Rachel jumped up and down, her face bright red. "My daddy is hurt. My daddy is hurt," she repeated over and over.

When their mother returned from shopping, she saw Sara standing beside an ambulance from St. Catherine's in front of their building. Several neighbors were peering out of their windows at the activity on the street.

"What's going on here?" Helen exclaimed. "Oh, my God! Sara! Are Robbie and Rachel OK?" She dropped her bag of groceries.

"It's Daddy, Ma. We're OK."

"What's happened to him?" Her mother's eyes opened wide.

"Take it easy, ma'am," the attendant said, as he began wheeling the gurney up to the apartment. "Your husband's finger got caught in a door. A doctor will sew it up. He'll be all right. Don't worry."

"Oh no! Where's Rachel? Where's Robbie?" her mother cried frantically.

"Rachel's upstairs with Robbie," Sara answered. "A nurse is with Daddy. She'll go with him to the hospital." Sara tried calming her mother with a hug. "Don't worry, Ma. Everything will be OK."

But then Sara, who had been trying so hard to act grown up, lost control of herself. She couldn't keep her feelings inside any longer. Her body began shaking, and her tears came rolling out. "I'm sorry, Ma. I'm so, so sorry. I didn't watch over everybody."

"Come here, *mamela*," Helen cried, hugging Sara tightly. "It's not your fault. It's too much for a little girl!" They stood there for several long moments, holding on to each other.

Finally Helen said, "Please, honey, help me pick up the groceries." They collected the items and began mounting the stairs. "Can you tell me what happened?" Helen asked calmly.

Feeling upset that she hadn't done more, Sara tried to find the right words. "Daddy began trembling in the living room. He went to the bathroom, and then he got angry at Rachel. Then he got very giddy. He was bringing us milkshakes, but he wasn't paying attention and he tripped, and the swinging door chopped his finger off."

"Oh, God in heaven," her mother said faintly. "What are we going to do?"

All Sara could think about was her failure. *Why don't I have the courage to speak to Daddy about his problem? If I had spoken to him, maybe I could have prevented the accident. Why hasn't Dr. Clayton helped Daddy? It really is up to me now. Somehow I have to tell Daddy, "We love you and we need you. We don't want you to be sick. For the sake of our family, please, please stop taking that terrible medicine that turns you into a wild person!" Am I too late? Too, too late?*

Chapter Five

As the day went on, Sara's distress turned to fantasy. She wanted to believe an alien invasion had caused the accident, not her father's sickness. She knew it was a strange idea, yet she couldn't put it out of her mind. Later that evening, when Helen sat with her at the kitchen table waiting for Josef's return from St. Catherine's Hospital, she asked Sara for more details about what had happened. Sara hesitated before answering.

"I know this sounds weird," she said at last, "but do you think Daddy is under some alien control? I haven't told you this, but I've been having nightmares for a couple of years about a masked man, someone who looks just like Daddy, who crawls inside him and takes over."

Helen looked at Sara incredulously. "Sara, dear, what kind of thoughts are those?"

"I mean, maybe some evil power swung the door onto Daddy's hand..." Sara stopped, realizing how bizarre that sounded.

"Sara, I don't think so. You have a lively imagination, *mamela*. Maybe you've been watching too many horror movies lately. But we do need to talk about your father's problem. You're ten, old enough to know about your father's condition. And you're old enough to keep private what's been happening. You know, it's just between us. You mustn't tell *anybody*."

Sara shifted nervously in her chair.

"Your father had the accident because he's still sick." She took Sara's hands in hers and looked into her eyes. "There is no masked man, Sara."

"But *why* is Daddy still sick?"

"Because he can't get out of the habit of taking the drug that makes him sick."

It took Sara a while to respond. "But I thought Dr. Clayton was helping him. I thought Daddy was getting better." Tears welled up in her eyes.

"We all thought that Dr. Clayton was helping your father—me, Grandma, Poppy, Uncle Irv. But your Daddy fooled us. He's been pretending that Dr. Clayton is helping him."

"But *why*? There must be a reason."

"He can't break the habit, so he doesn't want us interfering." She held Sara's hands and squeezed. "You know how you sometimes hide your Chunky chocolate wrappers under your pillow? And how, when I find them, you feel ashamed, because you know eating too many chocolates is bad for you?"

Sara nodded.

"Well, what your father takes is very, very bad for him. And he feels ashamed that we've found out that he's still taking it. But for his own good, we have to stop him!"

"Will he die if we don't stop him?"

"No, no, sweetheart. Daddy's not going to die. He's going to try harder to get well. We're going to help him."

"Do I *have* to talk to him?"

"What do you mean?"

"Well, Grandma told me I could make Daddy better if I spoke to him."

A pained look spread across Helen's face. "Oh, no! No, no, honey. Making Daddy better isn't your job. Grandma didn't mean that." She hugged Sara more tightly. "Daddy knows you love him. That's the most important thing."

"Do you still love Daddy?" Sara looked up at her mother, whose chin still held the scar from her father's bruises.

"Why, of course, I love Daddy, sweetheart. Why would you think..."

"You let Daddy go to the hospital all alone with the nurse. Why didn't you go with him?"

"Honey, I needed to stay with you and Robbie and Rachel." She looked at Sara with deep concern. "Don't worry. Uncle Irv's with Daddy. They'll be home later tonight."

"I want to stay up to see Daddy."

"But you have to be up for school in the morning."

"I need to see him, Ma," Sara said emphatically.

Uncle Irv dropped Josef back at the apartment just before midnight. "You get a good night's rest," Uncle Irv said, his arm around Josef's shoulder, as he helped him into the kitchen. "Don't worry about the store. We'll find a way to manage."

"Thanks, Irv," Josef said, patting him on the back with his still-good hand.

"Cup of coffee, Irv?" Ma said.

"Gotta run, Helen. It's late." He gave her a quick hug.

Josef was wearing a large bandage on his left middle finger. It resembled a giant finger-puppet, a ghost of gauze with a pot belly.

"Thank God you're home," Helen said with relief. "How's your finger?" She stared at the bandage and nervously pulled out a chair for him.

"My finger's just a stub now." He looked at Sara, whose eyes were bloodshot. "You should be sleeping, Sara."

"She's upset, Josef. And I'm upset." Helen was clasping and unclasping her hands. "The three of us need to be together right now. Sara needs to know the truth. And she needs to know we'll be OK."

He lowered his head and stared at the table.

"Josef, you're using heroin again, aren't you?" Helen's pain, anger, and disillusionment marched across her face.

Josef made a sound like a wounded animal. "I don't think Sara should hear this."

"But I want to know, Daddy."

No one said a word. Then her father looked up. "Clayton's a fraud, Helen."

"A fraud? What are you talking about?"

"The man's so high when I see him he can't get the syringe to work." Josef made a fist, pointed his forefinger, and pretended to shoot his left arm. Then he pointed to his eyes. "The man's got pinpricks for pupils."

What does Daddy mean? Sara was mystified.

"Are you accusing your doctor of taking drugs?" Helen burst out. "I'm talking about *you*, Josef. Are *you* using? Don't shift the blame to Clayton. Anyway, I don't believe you."

"If you saw him, you'd see for yourself, Helen. He's a *nebech*. But he's got all the drugs he needs because he's registered with the state."

"What's a *nebech,* Daddy?"

"A pitiful nothing of a person. I had his number from the get-go. Sara, I still say you shouldn't be here."

Sara looked at her mother for support.

"Your daughter needs to know what her father is doing to himself. She's crazy with questions, and so am I. What in the world does your doctor's problem have to do with you? For God's sake, why are *you* still taking drugs? What the hell is missing in your life? You have three beautiful children, a wife who loves you, a successful business, parents who dote on you. What more do you need?"

"I need…the stuff…to keep going!"

"I can't believe what you're saying. That stuff is killing you!"

"I need to work, Helen. Don't you understand? I have the butcher shop and you and the kids to take care of. Irv can't handle the business alone. And without using drugs, I simply can't work." He stared at his bandaged finger. "I'd be a basket case if I listened to Clayton. The fool wanted me on liver extract and vitamins, on rubdowns and whirlpool baths. Can you imagine? I told him I'd report him to the authorities if he didn't keep me going."

"So Clayton gave you drugs?"

"Morphine," he mumbled. "It's a painkiller. Less restricted legally than heroin."

"So now you're addicted to *morphine*?"

The tone of Helen's voice frightened Sara. She didn't know what morphine was. *Didn't Ma just say it was heroin that was hurting Daddy? Was morphine hurting him, too?*

"Morphine takes the edge off. Small doses, that's all."

Her mother's face turned white. "How do you think your parents will feel when they learn they've been paying a doctor to keep you on morphine?"

"Helen, you don't understand. At least with morphine I can work and come home to you and the kids. It tides me over... when I can't get shit."

Shit? Sara had heard the rough boys on Penn Street say, "Eat shit." *Why is Daddy talking like that?*

"So you're still using heroin, too!" Her mother's cry filled the room. "A year out of Lexington Hospital and you're still addicted to dope."

Shit? Dope? Sara was bewildered hearing all this, but too fearful to interrupt.

"Half an ounce," he said, shaking. "Twice a week. The cheapest on the street."

Helen's body went limp. "Oh, how could I not know?!" she wailed. "I'm the real dope. I leave you alone with the kids while you aren't in your right mind. I let them drive with you to the city while you're high. I leave them with you while you shoot up in the bathroom and then you maul your hand. How could I be so stupid?"

Josef squirmed in his seat but remained quiet.

"Too bad your daughter has to see you in this condition," Sara's mother said, weeping. "Can you feel good about that?"

Josef looked up sheepishly at Sara, and her eyes met his.

"I beg you, Josef," Helen pleaded. "You need to find a way out. Let us help you."

Sara couldn't understand. How could the father who just yesterday took her to Greenwich Village and taught her to accept all different kinds of people be the same father who was harming himself now? *Why doesn't Daddy stop taking "shit"? Why doesn't he just try—for my sake, for Robbie and Rachel's sake?*

Sara wished she had the right words, magic words that would make him turn away from "dope." Though she was angry at her father, part of her felt sorry for him, too. For the first time in her life, her father seemed not to be a grown man, but a child who did the same naughty thing again and again and refused to behave. It pained her deeply to see her father this way, and she longed for the loving father she used to know.

Chapter Six

THE FOLLOWING SATURDAY NIGHT, Sara lay awake in her bedroom, unable to sleep. She could hear the late-night buzz of her parents' voices in the kitchen. The next morning she found some brochures they had forgotten to put away. The brochures featured two treatments—methadone and shock therapy. Methadone, Sara read, was also addictive, and she remembered her parents rejecting it when her father came home from Lexington Hospital. She vaguely remembered them saying something about shock therapy too, and now here was a glossy pamphlet about a place in Connecticut called Hawthorne Lodge where shock therapy was being tried successfully. Sara wondered what "success" really meant. She could find nothing in the material to quiet her fears about the dangers of a person being "shocked."

"Is Daddy going to get treatment at Hawthorne Lodge?" Sara asked her mother that morning as they picked up the toys in the living room.

"Can't your father and I have some privacy? You've been listening in on our conversations again!" Helen said with a frown.

"No, Ma, I read the pamphlet," Sara said, looking at her mother with questioning eyes. "I'm worried, Ma!"

Helen put her arm around Sara. "I understand why you're

afraid, honey. We're only *considering* Hawthorne Lodge. Your father might be willing to try it."

"Isn't Daddy afraid of shock therapy?"

"He's cautious, honey. We need to know a lot more about it. Grandma and Poppy are coming over this morning to discuss it with us. They would have to pay for it, and it's expensive." Sara placed her brother and sister's games back in their toy chest. Her father had taken Robbie and Rachel around the corner to play with their cousin Ben. Sara moved around the living room on her hands and knees to check that none of Robbie's airplane models was hiding behind the couch or under the chairs. The familiar trail of her father's cigarette burns on the rug was glaringly noticeable. The stains reminded her again of the disappointment and sorrow her father had brought to the family. She wondered whether Grandma and Poppy had seen these telltale marks.

When they arrived, Hannah wanted to see Josef's hand right away. "Let me see what you did to yourself! Josef, show me your hand."

He extended his left arm and showed his mother the hand with the fat, bandaged finger. She took his hand in hers and studied the mass of cotton. "It's still bleeding," she cried.

"They're just stains," he responded.

"You had stitches?"

"Six of them."

"When do they come out?"

"In a week or so. It's not my whole hand, Ma. It's just a finger. I'll live. So don't worry." He drew his hand back, and with it he motioned for his parents to sit down in the living room.

"Josef's lucky it's just a finger," Helen said, hoping to calm her mother-in-law.

Hannah remained standing. Sara, who was watching and listening from the foyer, could see that her grandmother was upset. Hannah fixed her gaze on Helen. "How could you let him get away with it? How could you let Dr. Clayton pump Josef up with drugs! Dr. Clayton was supposed to be taking care of Josef!"

"How dare you blame me again! When are you going to face facts? Your son is the one with the problem, and he's a grown man. Ask *him* what happened. Give him some respect."

"*Nu*, well now," Poppy Mo chimed in. "What happened, son?"

"He's sick, that's what happened," Hannah continued. "He needs to be watched." She pointed her finger accusingly at Helen. "S*he* wasn't watching. She doesn't know how to care for our son!"

"Watch your words, Ma," Josef blasted back. "Helen's my wife, not my babysitter. She knows what I'm going through. You don't, so leave her alone. Now listen to me. We found a place that could help me. Maybe in no time my problem could be over."

"You found a place? Don't fool yourself, Josef. What kind of place? The last place Helen found in Kentucky, you were able to bribe some imbecile to get you drugs. We can't trust Helen. She didn't even notice you were still on heroin."

"How unfair you are!" Helen yelled. "I give Josef all my sympathetic understanding. You don't give him that. So Dr. Clayton turned out to be a fraud, but the right psychiatrist can help Josef, and we think there's a better one at the place we found."

"They found Hawthorne Lodge, Grandma!" Sara burst out, emerging from the foyer. "But...but they give people shocks there."

"What are you saying, Sara?" her father asked, worried.

"No more eavesdropping, young lady," Helen said. "You don't want more bad dreams, do you? Why don't you do your homework now? It's quiet in the bedroom with the children gone. We'll let you know when we come up with our plan."

"Let the child talk," Hannah said. "What are you saying, dear, about shocks?"

"She doesn't understand, Ma," Helen answered.

Josef bent down and put his good arm around Sara. "Sweetheart, please tell me what you're afraid of." And to Helen, he said quietly, "Let me take care of this."

"Aren't you afraid, Daddy...of being shocked?"

He shook his head, led Sara to the couch, and sat her next to him. He looked at Sara, then at his parents. "I want to explain our thinking to all of you." He reached for the Hawthorne Lodge brochure on the end table and handed it to Hannah. She and Mo sat in chairs side by side and read it.

"Helen and I agree," Josef continued. "Shock treatment is our last resort. It's a new way to treat addiction. We need to look into it more carefully, and I don't know if I'll qualify. They have to interview me—and *I* need to interview *them*. It's no small decision. The good part is I'll have a private doctor." He paused. "It's not at all like Lexington." A pained expression spread across his face. "The doctors were like jailers there. We need to visit Hawthorne Lodge to see what it's like."

"Look at these doctors," Mo said, passing the brochure to Hannah and pointing to the photos.

"I see this Dr. Lewis has won awards," Hannah said, looking at one of the five smiling men in white coats.

"He's the one I want," Josef said. "Now, can we discuss the pros and cons in more detail while Sara does her homework in the other room?"

Sara, feeling less agitated now, thought with relief, *Daddy's acting like a grown-up again.*

The plan, Sara later learned, was for Josef to visit Hawthorne Lodge Sanitarium, meet Dr. Lewis, the head psychiatrist, and then decide whether to take the treatment. Sara wanted to go with her family to Hawthorne Lodge, and Josef convinced Helen, who was reluctant, to allow it. "Seeing the place will dispel her bad dreams."

On the day of the trip, Josef had difficulty starting the Oldsmobile. He turned the key, but the engine just whirred and whirred without turning over. Finally, it started, and Hannah and Mo promised to buy him a new car once he finished the treatment.

"That's too much, Ma. Too much, Pa!"

"Let's see what happens, son," Mo said. "You can have something to look forward to." The conversation on the drive was about how Williamsburg was going downhill since Grandma and Poppy had moved to Queens. Josef objected to his parents speaking about *shvartzes* and *spics,* and he expressed hope that tensions wouldn't mount between these groups and the Hasidic Jews who also were moving in.

"So many children running wild in the streets, so many unfamiliar accents," Hannah said.

"Have you forgotten, Ma and Pa, that you were immigrants from Russia and you still have accents?" But then Josef praised his father for being the kind of landlord who did the *mitzvah* of renting the apartment above theirs to a Negro mother of three with nowhere else to go. "And isn't it nice that Mrs. Taylor's daughter, Ruth, has become Sara's good friend?"

"You'd like Mrs. Taylor and Ruth, Grandma," Sara said.

"Do you really think so?"

"Yes, because Mrs. Taylor knows how to sew and bake like you do, and she teaches Ruth how to sew and bake."

"Do you know what kinds of things they bake?'

"Hush puppies and sweet potato pie, and other things, too."

"I don't know anything about cakes like that, honey."

As Josef drove, Sara, who was sitting in the front seat with Helen, couldn't stop staring at her father's bandaged finger. She thought about Josef's accident, and his addiction to heroin that caused it. She wondered why no one said anything on the rest of the drive about the shock therapy her father might have. Was he afraid? Was everyone else too nervous to talk about what was in the future?

After a couple of more hours, they arrived at Hawthorne Lodge, a group of low, interlocking buildings on top of a knoll in a rural area. There was a large, expansive lawn in front of the buildings and a forest of tall trees behind it. Sara thought the lawn was big enough for Robbie to practice throwing his football, if Mom would ever allow him to come to Hawthorne Lodge. That is, if there would ever be a next time. She realized that Rachel was too young to come with them.

Sara's parents and grandparents left Sara with a nurse while they went to speak with the head psychiatrist. The nurse took Sara down three long hallways to the TV lounge. Breezeways with walls of glass connected numerous wings and laboratories, but Sara noticed there were no other people anywhere in sight. She wondered where everyone was.

The TV lounge was also deserted, although Sara noticed that the television, mounted high on the wall, was playing. She looked around at the plush couches, the paintings on the walls of vases of pink and blue flowers, and the potted plants sitting on the carpet.

"Where is everyone?" Sara asked the nurse.

"They're resting in their rooms, honey. When they're well enough, they'll watch TV. You can watch any show you want now." The nurse left the lounge after showing Sara how to change the channels.

Sara didn't realize she'd have to wait so long. She sat through *Search for Tomorrow, As the World Turns,* and *Beat the Clock*, but these shows were no more than images on the screen to her; she was focused on her parents' return and the news she would learn about her father. Finally, the family met her in the lounge and took her to lunch in the sanitarium restaurant. To Sara's surprise, the adults hardly exchanged any words. Seeing the sober expressions on their faces, she was hesitant to ask any questions. Maybe after meeting Dr. Lewis, they had decided against the treatment. Maybe her father was finally admitting his fears. *But if Daddy does consent to the treatment, will he have anyone to talk to in this place? Daddy could be very, very lonely at Hawthorne Lodge.*

As they drove away from the facility, Sara sat again between her father and mother. Everyone seemed to be waiting for her father to speak.

After a half hour or so of tense quiet, Josef finally spoke up. "I know Dr. Lewis said shock treatment won't be painful the way cold turkey was. But I'm afraid it will be the end of me."

"You mean you could die?" Sara blurted out.

"No, honey," her father added softly. "I'm not worried about dying. I'm afraid I won't be the same *me*. I'm afraid that my good memories will disappear along with my bad ones." Sara began to shiver, imagining her father with an empty brain, a brain as empty as the hallways and corridors at Hawthorne Lodge.

Then she began to think. *Would I give up my happy memories if I could make my bad memories disappear? Wouldn't it be great if I didn't remember my father hitting my mother, their nighttime fights, and my bad dreams? Would that mean, though, that I'd have no memories of Daddy loving me?*

Looking out the window, she began reading the highway signs to take her mind off her fears. "Groton," "New London," and "The Havens" were all new names to her. She saw that the stretch of road they were driving on was called the "Jewish War Veterans' Highway."

Spontaneously she shouted, "Look, Dad, this highway is named for Jewish soldiers! Are you a war veteran, Dad?"

"Yes, I am, Sara."

"Your father and all his friends enlisted in World War II, Sara," Poppy said.

"Do you want to keep your memories of the war, Dad?" Sara asked.

Josef hesitated. He placed his good arm around Sara's shoulder and called her by her nickname. "Sha-sha, it would take a lot for me to want to remember those times."

She liked the warmth of her father's touch and wished with all her might he didn't have to go away again. She felt a bit comforted when he finally said, "Well, maybe the treatment will be worth it. Maybe I'll have another chance at life."

"Hawthorne Lodge will cost a thousand a month," Poppy Mo called out from the backseat. "But if it can work for you, Josef, we'll spend whatever it takes to get you well again."

"You were right to encourage us to visit Hawthorne Lodge, Helen," Grandma said. "Dr. Lewis seems to know what he's talking about."

"I'm glad you think so, Ma."

"And I want to apologize for the things I said to you the other day," Grandma continued. "I was wrong to say the things I did. Will you forgive me?"

"Of course, Ma. We've all been very tense."

Hearing her mother and grandmother talk kindly to each other again, Sara's mood began to lift.

Chapter Seven

On the Sunday before he left for Hawthorne Lodge, Josef sat in the living room with Sara. "I'm going to be gone for several months, honey. Only your mother will be allowed to visit me. But I want you to know I'm going to be OK. Do you hear me?"

"How can you know for sure?" Sara asked.

"You love me, don't you?"

Sara nodded.

"Well, that's how I know. I'll pull through because of you, Sha-sha. And because of Mom, and Robbie and Rachel."

"What *is* shock therapy, Daddy?"

Josef began stroking Sara's hair. He paused and looked into her eyes. "Dr. Lewis says he can touch the part of my brain that contains my memories of heroin. By touching those memories, he can make them disappear. And so my craving can disappear."

"How can Dr. Lewis touch the memories in your brain?" Sara laughed nervously. "Does he have a magic wand?"

"He touches the brain...with electricity," he answered solemnly.

Images of Dr. Frankenstein experimenting on his monster flashed through Sara's mind, from a movie she and Robbie watched on TV. She wanted to ask her father more questions.

She wanted to know why he couldn't get better by himself without shock treatments. Why couldn't he just stop taking heroin on his own so he wouldn't have to leave the family? She wanted to remind him of what he originally told Ma, that he would stop taking heroin himself when he was good and ready.

"Aren't you ready yet?" she wanted to ask. "You know heroin is bad for you." But she just couldn't get those words out. "Why can't I visit you *with* Mom?" she asked instead. "I'm your daughter. I'm ten, a preteen!"

"I wish you could, but I told you, children aren't allowed."

Sara frowned. "But I'll need proof that you're OK!"

"Mom will let you know, Sara."

"But Mom likes to keep secrets," she answered, snuggling closer to him on the couch. "Dad, can you write me letters? You can give them to Mom. That way I'll know for sure you're all right."

"Letters? I guess I could. But when the treatment kicks in, I may have to stop writing."

"How long will the treatment take?" Sara asked, holding on to him tightly.

"About six months. But it could be more," he replied. "It's a long process, honey. They have to orient me…run tests. Then, the treatments and the follow-up. Uncle Irv will take care of the butcher shop while I'm away, like he did when I went to Lexington."

"Oh, Dad," she cried. "So long!"

"I'll do my best to write, sweetheart," Josef promised.

Sara's bad dreams returned, only now, the scary figure causing her to awaken at night resembled Boris Karloff, the actor who played Dr. Frankenstein's monster, with stitches on his forehead and his leg dragging chains.

By the time the shock treatments began, summer had ended. Helen visited Hawthorne Lodge once every two weeks with Uncle Nat, who drove her there. Sometimes she was able to see Josef, but sometimes she wasn't. That's because, as she told Sara, every case is different, and after a treatment, Josef could be in good spirits and want company, or he could be sad and want to be alone. But whether she did actually see Josef or just spoke with Dr. Lewis, she brought a letter home to Sara that Josef had written, and Sara wrote one back.

> September 25, 1957
> Dear Sha-sha,
> Did I ever tell you about courage? That's what you have when you're frightened to do something that's right, but you do it anyway. I can't lie to you and say I'm not afraid of shock therapy, but I'm having the treatment because it's the right thing to do. I want to be courageous. How about you? Is there something you want to do that you're afraid of? Can you be courageous? Write to me about it.
> *Love, Dad*

> October 1, 1957
> Dear Dad,
> I think I was courageous in school. We put on

a skit about the Negro students in Little Rock, Arkansas, who want to go to Little Rock Central High. We had to choose sides and play different parts. I volunteered to be one of the white kids protesting outside the school when the Negro students wanted to enter. I started shouting through a megaphone, "Let them in! We're all human beings, in the same boat." Remember? That's what you told me and Robbie when you took us to Greenwich Village and we saw Negro and white people holding hands. Well, one of my classmates didn't like what I said and shouted at me, "Hey, there are no whites at Little Rock Central High who want the Negro kids in their classes." And I answered, "Well, there should be, because that would be the right thing to do." Was that courage, Dad?
Love, Sha-sha

October 30, 1957
Dear Sha-sha,
I'm proud of your courage! Keep it up. I'm tired now. Need to rest.
Love, Dad

November 5, 1957
Dear Dad,
I hope you get your energy back, because there's something on my mind. I think it's the opposite

> of courage. It happened to me when you lost the tip of your finger in the foyer. I didn't have the courage to help you right away. I just stood and watched Robbie call the ambulance. And more important, Dad, I've never had the courage to talk to you about your problem, and how bad it makes me feel. I'm sorry. Does that ever happen to you? You know the right thing to do, but you can't do it? I sure can use your help with this one. Can I write more to you about it next time?
> *Love, Sha-sha*

When Helen returned home in late November from a visit to Hawthorne Lodge, she looked sad, but her voice was hopeful. "Daddy has a slight twitch on the right side of his face," she told Sara. "And he's having trouble remembering some things. He thinks he's forgotten how to spell. But it's still too soon to tell. Don't be frightened, honey. It's temporary. His letter is… well, it's short this time. Dr. Lewis said he's going to pick right up."

This time there was no date on Josef's letter.

> Deer Saa-saa,
> Love yu. Alwayz. Nest time be better.
> *Dad*

Sara thought his letter seemed like it had been written by a child. *How can Ma trust what Dr. Lewis says? Why isn't she upset like me? What's happened to my daddy?*

Sara sat down at the kitchen desk and took out a sheet of paper from her notebook. How could she write to her father without letting him know how worried she felt? But she had to, she *must!* Out of love for her father. Isn't that also courage?

Chapter Eight | 1957–1958

A week later, her mother had bad news for Sara. Over breakfast, she said, "Dr. Lewis says letter writing puts too much strain on Daddy. Honey, it will be best to postpone your writing until Daddy's shock treatments are completed and he's in rehab." This news was a huge disappointment to Sara and caused her to brood constantly over her father's condition. Her disturbing dreams continued, her headaches returned, and she found herself eating too much.

When *exactly* would her father go into rehab, Sara wanted to know, and what would his days *there* be like? She thought of him walking down the long, empty hallways of Hawthorne Lodge looking for someone to talk to. She pictured him hearing the sounds of voices, following the sounds to the TV lounge, but finding the lounge empty with the TV playing for no one. Would her father be watching shows like *You Bet Your Life* and *The Honeymooners*—and would he still be laughing at them the way he used to?

Only at school could Sara distract herself from her worries and sadness. She imagined her father would be pleased if she applied herself and did well in school. In Miss Brown's fifth-grade class, the students were debating whether the United States should build up its missile program, since the Russians were winning the Space Race. The Russians had just sent up

Sputnik 2 with the street dog Laika inside, while the United States was pining over the failure of the Vanguard. Many students felt disappointed by their country's poor performance.

When Miss Brown asked who wanted to represent her class in the school-wide assembly program on the Soviet Challenge, Sara knew she had to volunteer. She was already troubled by the fact that schools in New York City were preparing for the possibility of a nuclear bomb attack with shelter drills and the distribution of dog tags. Sara remembered her father's distress when she asked him if he wanted to remember World War II. She felt strongly that if countries competed to build bigger and better missiles, the world could break out into war again and everyone would be in great danger. Sara wanted to share her point of view in the assembly even though it was not popular among her classmates. Meanwhile, every night, she remembered her father, but also the whole world in her prayers. She pleaded with God to bless her father, her family, and all of outer space.

Sara's best friend in Miss Brown's class was Ruth Taylor, her upstairs neighbor. Ruth agreed that all the talk about the Soviet menace was bringing the country down and said she'd try to help Sara get votes to be the class representative at the assembly. The person taking a position against Sara was Robert Goldman, the most handsome and popular boy in class. Sara herself had a crush on him. He had, in fact, invited Sara to attend his birthday party before the plans for the Soviet Challenge Assembly had been announced. Now though, when Robert saw Sara in class, he no longer engaged her in conversation. She wondered what had happened to their budding relationship. Finally, on the way out of school one afternoon before the vote, she mustered the courage to ask him why he was being so unfriendly.

"Why do you have to speak to the whole school about your political views?" was his response.

"What's wrong with speaking out?" she said.

"It just doesn't appeal to me." And after a moment of hesitation, he added, "Boys are supposed to speak out, not girls."

Robert's words gave Sara a bad feeling, and she walked away.

Later, when she told Ruth what Robert had said, Ruth responded that Sara shouldn't feel bad about Robert's rejection. "Who'd want a boyfriend like that, anyway?" she said. "Don't you want a boyfriend who encourages you to speak your mind?"

The assembly went well. Sara received sufficient votes to speak for Miss Brown's class. Ruth had encouraged a majority of the class, including all the girls, to vote for Sara. Ruth said a girl's voice needed to be heard, and Sara was the only female candidate. At the assembly, several sixth-grade boys who spoke wanted the United States' missile program to be beefed up so that the country could rise up out of its slump. Sara said that the best thing for the world to do about space projects would be to turn them over to the United Nations, because then countries would not be in competition with one another. She quoted Eleanor Roosevelt to stress her point. "Before we drift into war…the United Nations…should be called into play…. The mobilization of world opinion and methods of negotiation should be developed and used by every nation…

to strengthen the United Nations…to prevent war." Sara was surprised when she got a round of applause.

Two months later, when the cars parked on Penn Street were topped with snow, Sara was greatly cheered by her mother's words to her and Robbie. "Your father's recuperating. He's in rehab."

"Will he be coming home soon?" Sara asked.

"Not quite yet, dear," Helen answered.

"Why? Doesn't Daddy want to see us?"

"Right now, dear, your father doesn't know what he wants. But Dr. Lewis, who sees your father every day, thinks he's not ready to come home."

"Dr. Lewis isn't Daddy! How do you know Dr. Lewis isn't hiding something?"

"Calm down, Sara. The doctor isn't hiding anything. Daddy still has bad days. Dr. Lewis wants us to wait until he's on a more even keel."

"How can you know for sure if you haven't actually seen Daddy?"

"Please, honey, don't get so upset. I don't want to worry about you, too. I'll speak to Dr. Lewis."

Helen kept her promise. A few days later, Sara overheard her mother on the phone asking Dr. Lewis when Josef might be ready to come home. The doctor told her Josef needed more peace and quiet to build up his strength.

It actually took several more months of recuperation before Josef returned. When he finally arrived home on Penn Street in December 1958, he had been away for a year. Sara felt that her prayers finally had been answered.

The moment Josef walked in the door with Uncle Nat, who had driven him home from Hawthorne Lodge, Sara could read the disappointment on her father's face. She saw the worry lines on his brow. But a smile spread over his face when, tilting his head, he fixed his gaze on her, Robbie, and Rachel. "My beautiful children!" he exclaimed, opening his arms. They ran to him, and he covered them in hugs and kisses. Sara saw tears in his eyes.

"How are you, Daddy?" she asked.

He didn't answer. Still holding his children, he looked up at Helen and pointed to his head. "Big holes in there," he whispered. "Important people, events—gone."

Hearing his words, Sara strained to hear what else he was saying.

"I hate to say this," he whispered to Helen. "It's worse than cold turkey."

Uncle Nat put his arm around Josef. "C'mon, buddy, you're home, back with your family. Cheer up!" He turned to Helen. "Why not take out the schnapps, Helen, so we can drink to Josef's homecoming?"

Helen took out a bottle of whisky and three tiny schnapps glasses. Nat said as they drank, "To you, Josef, and your family, to Katz and Block Kosher Meats, and to life, *l'chaim!*"

As happy as Sara was to see him, Josef was not the father she was hoping to see. He looked lost and confused. For one thing, when Robbie presented him with his harmonica, he turned it around in his hands as if it were a strange object. Robbie then took the instrument from him and started blowing into it.

Josef asked for it again and started playing the first few notes of "Yankee Doodle." But he couldn't continue. He returned the harmonica to Robbie and sat down quietly. Becoming sullen, he let his head fall onto his chest.

The next few days, Josef slept for long periods, sometimes waking in the afternoons and feeling too groggy to go to work. The winter cold seemed to discourage him, too. But by the end of the week, he told Helen that even if he felt too weak, he would have to push himself. He couldn't dawdle any longer and leave all the business for Uncle Irv. Soon he was back to work. But he was also back to his strange patterns: leaving home at three-thirty in the morning, missing family dinners, coming home after ten, and falling asleep in the living room club chair rather than in the bedroom with Helen.

One cloudy afternoon in late December shortly after Josef resumed working, Sara came home from school and saw her mother in the kitchen bent over the stove. She was mixing the contents of a steaming pot, staring into it and breathing heavily. Sara dropped her books on the desk. Helen stood fixed in her spot, mechanically turning the spoon in the large pot.

"I'm home, Ma. What's wrong?"

Helen lifted her head. Sara could see beads of perspiration on her forehead. "I don't know where to turn, who to talk to," she said in a voice so faint, Sara could hardly hear her.

"It's Daddy, isn't it?"

Helen wiped her reddened hands on her apron and sat down at the kitchen table. "I shouldn't be talking to you about this..."

"You can talk to me, Ma."

Helen's eyes were pools of sadness. "I can't turn to Annette anymore. I've worn out her shoulder with my crying."

Taking a seat at the table, Sara reached for her mother's hand.

Helen tried holding back her tears. "Nothing's worked for your father. Not cold turkey, not Dr. Clayton, not shock therapy. Your father realizes now that no one knows how to cure him. And he's given up trying to help himself. Who knows how long he'll be able to work?"

"No one can help him? I can't believe it!" Sara felt an overwhelming pity for her father who had tried so many ways to get better. "But why is Daddy spending so little time at home? We hardly see him when he's not at work."

"He's scrounging for drugs!" Helen burst out. "That's why."

"But he just got back from the sanitarium!"

Helen rose from her chair, walked to the window, and looked out. It was beginning to pour. "He told me every cell in his body still craves that poison. That's why he doesn't come home. He's finding ways to satisfy his habit."

Sara was horrified to think that her father was still addicted. "Why can't Daddy get better? Do you know why nothing is helping him? Don't other people with his problem ever get better?" Her mother began trembling. It seemed to Sara she was too upset to speak. But then she let it slip out, "Maybe he can't get better because he's been sick for so long. Too long. He was in deep trouble even before we got married."

"Weren't you just teenagers then?" A memory of a terrible argument between her mother and grandmother flashed through Sara's mind. She recalled dangerous places called "clubrooms" and a name, the Moonglow.

Helen began to sob. "Oh, I never meant to bring this up again. God should forgive me."

Sara suddenly remembered something else. Someone named Spencer. Her father had come under his influence. *Who were Spencer and the other Moonglow boys? Why didn't I question Ma back then about them?* An old sense of guilt surfaced with a new strength. *Maybe if I had spoken to Daddy long ago, like Grandma had asked...maybe if I had insisted that Daddy not take that package of drugs from the Negro man in Greenwich Village...maybe I should talk to Daddy now...*

Regret enveloped her. And though realizing how young her father was when he became addicted depressed Sara, she also felt, in an odd way, that a heavy curtain was being raised, a dark veil was being lifted. Before she was even born, her father had his problem. It finally sunk in. Her father didn't just get sick three years ago when she was eight years old and began witnessing his strange behavior. No. There were deeper things in her father's past—things she needed to know. So many questions raced through her mind: *What happened to Daddy back then? Did he have difficulty in his family? Was it bad friends? A gang?*

"Oh, Mom," she cried out, "how, how did Daddy get involved with drugs? I have to know!"

Helen put her head down on the table. "I shouldn't have said anything. I'm expecting Annette to bring the kids back any minute. They must be stuck in the rain."

"They're not here yet. Tell me what happened to Daddy!"

"No more today, Sara. Not now, and not tomorrow either. I need to wait until you're old enough. I wouldn't be a good mother otherwise."

"When will I be old enough?"

"It's not a matter of years," she said, looking up. "When you're ready, I'll know it. And then I'll tell you."

Sara looked directly into her mother's eyes. "Will you promise to tell me?"

"Yes, but only when I think you're ready."

Sara met her aunt in the foyer as Annette rushed into the apartment with the children, who were completely soaked. She inhaled the aromas wafting through the apartment and said with a smile, "I can smell your mother's beef and barley soup."

"We want soup!" Rachel began chanting. Robbie and Ben joined her like parrots, and the three of them started giggling.

Annette, seeing Sara's forlorn look, asked, "What's the matter, *mamela*?"

"Ma says I'm not old enough."

"For what?"

"To know how my father first got sick."

"Oh, that's hard for her."

Helen shouted from the kitchen, "Is that you, Annette?"

"*Ssh*. Please don't tell my mother I'm complaining," Sara whispered, as they headed to the kitchen.

Chapter Nine | 1959

During the week that followed, Helen began smoking more than usual, forgot about the food cooking on the stove and burned it, and complained about losing important papers. She yelled at Sara for the slightest reasons.

"How do you expect anyone else to use this space?" she screamed one evening after dinner, pointing to Sara's textbooks and notebooks covering the kitchen desk. "Take your things away! A twelve-year-old should know how to clean up after herself. I need to work there, too!" Then she lit a cigarette and began to cry.

Instead of feeling angry, Sara was worried. She wondered what was upsetting her mother and making her act this way. *Is Grandma blaming Ma again? Does Grandma want Daddy to have more shock therapy? Did Dr. Lewis turn her down because Daddy's been addicted too long? I wish Ma would tell me more. I guess she doesn't think I'm ready yet. But I need to know! I'm afraid to talk to her about this again, but maybe I should anyway.*

To please her mother, she cleared away her school books and papers, tossing all of them in her school bag, except for her history book. Sara was too upset to do her history homework that night, so she placed the book on a corner of the kitchen desk, where she would easily notice it in the morning.

She'd finish her assignment before she left for school.

She was awakened at around three-thirty in the morning by her father's bathroom sounds. The clink of his paraphernalia in the sink saddened her. *He's at it again,* she thought. She fell back to sleep, but tossed and turned fitfully. By 5 a.m. Sara got up. In the dim light, through the bedroom window, she could see an ominous mass of clouds hovering in the winter sky. A voice in her head said, "He'll never recover," even though she tried her best to shut the voice out.

She entered the kitchen in her bathrobe, sat at the desk, and riffled through the pages of her history book. The others were still asleep, and the kitchen felt cozy and quiet. Inside her history book, like a bookmark, she was surprised to find a letter addressed to "Ma." The page was written in a rough hand, her mother's, with many cross-outs, as if her mother had been trying to figure out what she really wanted to say. *Ma was so upset, she probably didn't realize she put the letter in my textbook,* Sara thought.

> Ma,
>
> I ~~cannot accept~~ am torn up by your idea that Josef and I take an extended vacation in Florida without the children. I know Dr. Lewis recommends a *complete* change for Josef, but for him and me to move, without the kids, like you suggest, is out of the question too much for me to bear. ~~You'll have to find someone else to go with him.~~ I realize you're being generous in giving Josef a new car and offering to pay expenses, but I can't leave my children. There has to be something else we can

> do to break Josef's habit! But to leave my kids? It's too much to ask. I can't do it. ~~Give me time!~~

Sara felt like exploding. *Grandma wants Ma and Daddy to move away and leave me, Robbie, and Rachel alone! Why is Grandma being so mean? How can Ma call Grandma "generous" if she wants Ma and Daddy to move away from us? Is Daddy's problem OUR fault?* With all these questions swirling in her mind, Sara resolved again to confront her mother.

But when her mother appeared in the kitchen doorway, about to brew her coffee, she immediately said, "I need to talk to you, Sara. Grandma and Poppy want Daddy and me to take a vacation."

"A vacation? Is that what you call it?" Sara couldn't hold back her anger.

"What do you mean, Sara?"

"You're going to move away with Daddy and leave your own children behind!"

"Oh my God! Where did you get that idea?"

"From your letter." Sara waved the letter like a flag. "I found it in my history book."

"Oh, what a blunder on my part! I'm like a chicken without a head! Listen to me, Sara. I was just scribbling my thoughts down—trying to sort my feelings out so I could accept what has to be done. We have to do something to help your father. You don't know the full story."

"So what *is* the full story? What has to be done? And what's going to happen to us if you leave? Are you going to place us in an orphanage?" Sara stomped around the kitchen looking for...something...anything. In her upset, she took a jar of peanut butter out of the refrigerator, then slammed the door shut and stood at the table. With her finger, she spooned out a wad of peanut butter, began licking her "lollipop," and cried out: "Why are you punishing *us*?"

"You crazy girl, no one is punishing you. Come here, sweetheart. Let me give you a hug." Helen wrapped her arms around Sara and held her tightly. "Please, dear, sit down." Seating herself opposite Sara, she sighed deeply. "You know how much...how much I've been worrying about your father. Grandma and I have been discussing Daddy's relapse with Dr. Lewis. He thinks there may still be some time for us to save the positive effects of the shock therapy. But to do that, Daddy's got to change his whole environment so his old patterns and memories don't return."

Sara pouted and pointed her peanut butter finger in the air first one way, then another. "Daddy's got to do this, Daddy's got to do that. Is he a child? You and Grandma treat him as if *he* were the twelve-year-old, not me!"

"Don't be sarcastic, Sara. I'm trying to explain. You're making it harder for me! Are you going to listen or not?"

Reluctantly Sara nodded.

"Grandma calls the move a vacation," Helen continued. "She and Poppy think Daddy's working much too hard after all he's gone through, so they want him to take a rest. But mostly, they think a vacation might bring about the change Dr. Lewis is advising."

"Grandma says this, Grandma says that." Sara couldn't stop herself from parroting. "Is that what *you* want, Ma? It sure didn't sound that way in your letter."

Finally Sara's questions seemed to touch a nerve. Her mother broke down and cried, her words coming through loud sobs. "It's so hard for me to think about leaving you kids. I've been agonizing over it, Sara—but I'd have to go with your father. He can't be alone. And there's no other solution I can think of! Your father is getting worse and worse. I can't just watch him fall apart. We've exhausted every treatment, every known medication…except for that new drug, methadone. But your father won't hear of it. It's experimental, and he's already too damaged by experiments and too afraid. I feel so trapped, because there's nothing else we can do." She paused, shook her head back and forth, and wiped her wet eyes with a tissue. "I hate to death to admit it, but maybe a vacation could be good for Daddy."

"How long of a vacation?"

"A few months," Helen said, swallowing hard. "Daddy needs to form new habits and get used to a drug-free life."

Sara let out a gasp. "That's a long time."

"I know, Sara, honey. It breaks my heart." She took Sara's hand in hers. "The consolation is that when we come back, you'll have a daddy who's better."

"Florida is so far away," Sara said. She suddenly remembered the voice in her head saying he'd never recover.

"Yes, honey, it's far. But Daddy's sickness might go away if he has a chance to relax in a beautiful new location. Grandma believes that things can improve sometimes if you change your place. Maybe she's right. She reminded me I have an aunt and uncle in Florida who can help us find an apartment and show us around."

"An apartment?" The thought of living in an apartment

gave Sara an idea. "If you have an apartment, we can live with you! We can go with you."

Helen looked lovingly at Sara. "I wish with all my heart, Sara dear, that we could take you all along. But we can't. You and Robbie have school. We don't want your lives disrupted."

"But who will take care of us?" Sara heard the rain that began lashing against the kitchen window.

"I've asked Aunt Annette and Uncle Nat. They want you to live with them." Helen lifted Sara's chin and kissed her forehead. "Your cousin Ben would love it. He and Robbie have such good times with each other. And you can be a big help to your aunt with looking after Rachel." Helen's eyes began to tear again. "Look, dear, it's not really a vacation. We're only calling it that to get your father to like the idea. He didn't want to go at first. Grandma, Poppy, and I had to coax him."

"Why...*why* didn't Daddy want to go?" Surely, her mother was withholding important information. She heard a warning voice in her head. *If you let him go now, he may never return.* Sara hoped with all her might that her father would reject this plan to leave her, Robbie, and Rachel behind. After all, he'd been home from Hawthorne Lodge only a short time.

"Daddy didn't want to go," her mother continued, "because he's afraid his sickness will just follow him down there, and he'll be sick in a strange, new place."

"Well, isn't that a good reason for him *not* to go?" Sara said.

"It's not a good enough reason, Sara. Daddy's just getting sicker and sicker *here*."

Her father's bathroom sounds that morning confirmed that her mother spoke the truth.

"There's a chance that a new environment will help him," her mother continued. "We'll drive down to Florida in the Cadillac Grandma and Poppy gave to Daddy. He'll be free of all his usual routines, all the demands of the business. We'll visit hotels, eat in restaurants, and even go dancing together, like we used to."

"You make it sound like fun, Mommy. But you're going away from us! Robbie and I can go to school in Florida." Sara had the idea that if only she, Robbie, and Rachel went to Florida, too, she could prevent the catastrophe the voice in her head was warning her about.

"I'm so sorry, honey." Helen tried to hold back more tears. "It may sound like fun, but it's not. It's a recuperation period for your father, to see if he can become healthy without using drugs." She pulled herself together. "Listen to me, dear. When Daddy gets better, we can all go to Florida as a family."

"So you *will* let me and Robbie transfer schools?"

"We'll go..." Helen hesitated, "for a short time...during your school break."

"You're just saying that. You'll never take us to Florida. And you're never coming back. You're abandoning us!" Sara yelled, becoming more upset by the moment.

"Now you've got to listen to me, Sara," Helen said firmly. "I know it's hard for you to understand that Daddy and I have to leave you...temporarily. God knows it's hard for me to believe it has to be done, too. My heart is torn. But there's really no alternative. I've thought about it over and over. With your aunt and uncle who love you, you kids will be safe. You'll be in the same schools, and before you know it, we'll be back.

You're a smart girl, Sara, and you must understand I wouldn't be doing this if I didn't think it was absolutely necessary, so that you, Robbie, and Rachel *can* have a father in your lives. In the meantime, we'll call you every single night on the telephone and tell you everything we're doing." After a moment of silence, she added, "I've been torturing myself with this decision for days."

Sara walked to the window. The rain blurred everything. She was feeling more and more resentful that she had a sick father and that his illness was consuming not only him but the whole family. Everything revolved around her father and his problem. And no matter what they did, he wasn't getting better. And now he was taking her mother away with him and away from her. "Ma, how did Daddy ever become so sick like this in the first place? You promised to tell me when I was old enough. You've got to tell me!"

Helen's lip quivered. "We'll see, Sara. Maybe when we're back from Florida, you'll be ready, and I'll be ready, too."

Sara tried hard not to cry. She hated the way her mother kept secrets. She walked over to the kitchen door, removed the calendar that hung there, and held it up before her mother. "Ma, I want you to mark the day in red that you'll be coming back home."

Chapter Ten

A "few months" turned out to be many more. By September, Sara counted eight months of separation from her parents. No longer distracted by the newness of her life with her aunt and uncle, Sara felt overwhelmed by insecurity and deprivation. In Aunt Annette and Uncle Nat's apartment, there was no desk for Sara to do her homework. She missed having her own bed. Instead, she and Rachel slept in the living room on an uncomfortable convertible couch, while Robbie slept on a cot in his cousin Ben's room. Rachel woke Sara every morning by jumping up and down on the mattress. Sara tried to stop her sister's acrobatics, but Rachel couldn't control herself, and Sara didn't want to physically pin her down. When Sara complained to her aunt, Annette said the child needed to let off steam. Her aunt's leniency felt like neglect to Sara. *What about my feelings?* Sara thought. Uncle Nat didn't have a big say in things either. He worked long hours as a house painter and was home to spend time with the children only on the weekends.

The telephone calls from her mother came frequently at first from a place called Coconut Grove, but not every evening as Helen had promised. "We're just getting situated, darling," her mother told her. "When everything's set up, you'll hear from us more regularly." Often, when Sara asked to speak to her father, Helen said he was sleeping and couldn't come to the phone. *What is Ma keeping from me?* Sara grew more and more suspicious.

"Mom, could you please call *before* Daddy falls asleep? I need to talk to him!" Even when she did talk to her father, though, he didn't have much to say, and he always sounded groggy.

"Are you sick, Daddy? I'm worried."

"No, honey, just tired."

His lack of energy made Sara realize what a big toll his illness already had taken on him, and she feared that her parents would have to be gone a long time before her father actually showed signs of improvement. After these telephone conversations, Sara missed being with her parents even more.

By escaping into schoolwork, as she had in the past, Sara forgot for a while about the crowded and chaotic home situation at Aunt Annette's. She loved her seventh-grade English class because her teacher, Miss Heller, a short woman in her forties with curly brown hair, encouraged the class to discuss interesting books she called "allegories," such as *Animal Farm, Gulliver's Travels,* and *Candide.* Sara enjoyed offering her comments and opinions, and she liked hearing the comments of other students. She remained enthusiastic about the class until Miss Heller announced their new unit, the biographies of significant people who had handicaps, people like Hans Christian Andersen, Madame Curie, and Helen Keller. Sara felt sorry for people with handicaps, but reading about them made her feel uncomfortable. "Why do we have to read about people with such problems?" she asked in class, feeling her own problems were already too much for her to handle.

"What people without problems would you suggest we read about?" Miss Heller responded.

Sara thought for a few minutes. She felt put on the spot, but on the other hand, she was glad Miss Heller was drawing her out. It was hard for Sara to understand the discomfort she was feeling, but she wanted to understand herself better. She felt she could trust Miss Heller and be honest with her, even in front of the class. Sara remembered the woman in the public eye whom she admired the most. "I'd like to read about Eleanor Roosevelt."

"I'm glad you mentioned Mrs. Roosevelt. We will read about her soon, Sara, and when we do, I think you'll be surprised to learn that her life is very different than what you might imagine." Sara wondered what Miss Heller knew about Eleanor Roosevelt's life, but she was sure that whatever it was, the information would be helpful.

On the long walk home from Middle School 318, Sara told Ruth that she didn't think handicapped people wanted to make their handicaps widely known. "Didn't President Roosevelt hide his polio problem?"

Ruth smiled. "Maybe," she said. "But I think disadvantages make people stronger. When we learned about President's Roosevelt's handicap, didn't we admire him more? If we don't know about people's limitations, we might think their successes come easily, when they don't."

Impressed by Ruth's words, Sara stopped in her tracks. "You're making me think, Ruth."

"I've got a handicap," Ruth said, "in case you haven't noticed." She pointed to her own dark skin. "At least in this country it's a handicap."

Sara felt embarrassed. "I think I know what you mean," she answered.

"I started reading about Helen Keller a long time ago," Ruth continued. "Her story helped me see that people who are looked down upon can overcome their feelings of inferiority."

"I guess lately, with my parents gone, I've been feeling handicapped, too," Sara said. "And I've been feeling sorry for myself. Maybe I need to look at my situation differently."

"You know that *my* dad is also gone. He doesn't live with us anymore," Ruth said, a few tears beginning to fall.

Sara nodded. "I knew your father didn't live with you. But I never wanted to pry."

"He left our family," Ruth said, looking down at the sidewalk, "after our apartment house in Harlem burned down, shortly before we moved into your grandfather's building."

"Your building burned down? How did that happen?"

"We never found out. It was in the papers. They called the building a 'fire trap' and said the landlord didn't keep it up right. My mom didn't think we'd ever survive without my dad's income, but she was lucky to find that job at St. Catherine's as a nurse and take in sewing jobs at home. And your grandfather, Sara. Without him, we'd never have found an apartment that we could afford."

Sara had to digest this new information: Ruth, her best friend, had been living in an unsafe apartment house, her father had abandoned her family, and her mother survived on her own, taking care of Ruth and her two brothers. *What a story!* Sara wondered why Ruth's father had left, but she didn't dare ask Ruth anything else. After all, following her own mother's insistence, Sara had never shared her father's story with Ruth either.

Ruth's courage helped Sara regain her own. She remembered her father's letters to her about courage when he was going through shock therapy at Hawthorne Lodge, and how she herself had defended the Negro students who were integrated into the Little Rock schools when she was in the fourth grade.

"Hey, Ruth," she said. "When were you the bravest you've ever been?"

Ruth looked at her and started giggling. "Today."

"You're kidding, right? What's so funny?"

"Today I asked George Herman to help me with my math homework."

"But you're a whiz at math. Why do you need..."

Ruth looked at Sara slyly. "You know how shy George is."

"Uh-huh."

"He would've never asked me out to get a soda."

"That *is* courage you've got, girl!" Sara said, and they laughed the rest of the way home.

When Miss Heller introduced the next reading unit—about the discrimination and anti-Semitism that resulted in the Holocaust—Sara began to identify with Anne Frank. After each reading assignment in Anne's diary, Miss Heller asked her students to write their responses. Sara wrote that she could imagine how Anne felt when her father, Mr. Frank, lost his spice business, and she and her family had to live in fear in a crowded attic with the Van Daan family. "I'm also living in fear. My parents are gone, I'm living in a small apartment with my sister, brother, aunt, uncle, and cousin, and I don't know for sure if my parents will ever come back." Miss Heller wrote in the margin: "Sara, I'm very sorry your parents had to leave you for a while. You're a very intelligent and resourceful student with a questioning mind. Writing about your feelings is a good idea. Your parents will be proud of your compositions when they return."

Miss Heller's words filled Sara with greater confidence. She admired her teacher greatly, not only because it was obvious that she loved teaching but also because she expected wonderful things from her students. She said she viewed them to be the future leaders of the world, including the girls. Sara remembered how bad she'd felt when Robert Goldman, the boy she had a crush on in fifth grade, didn't think girls should speak out in public. And she felt especially curious about Miss Heller when she admitted to the class one day that she hadn't wanted to get married, though she regretted not having children of her own. Sara was impressed that Miss Heller didn't see her single, childless situation as a tragedy. She had created another purpose in life for herself besides being a wife and mother. Thinking about Miss Heller's courage helped Sara to sustain her own feelings of optimism and good cheer, but whenever she found herself missing her parents, she'd sink down again into the dumps.

The next time Sara spoke to her mother on the phone, she told her she was reading about Anne Frank. "Anne had to live in a cramped apartment like me. And then she got taken to Bergen-Belsen and died there."

"Oh, honey, please don't compare yourself to Anne Frank. Anne Frank wasn't living in a free, safe country like you are. You may feel sad that you and your brother and sister are living with Aunt Annette and Uncle Nat, but Daddy and I won't be gone forever, and you have your whole life ahead of you. Your mother and father are both alive, and we both love you."

"Well, sometimes I just feel bad." Sara paused. "I miss you and Daddy so much. You've been gone so long. And you hardly ever let me speak to Daddy. Is he getting better? Sometimes I think *he* is going to die."

"No, Sara, he's not going to die. I don't want you to worry like this."

"But is Daddy getting better or not? Why won't you tell me?"

"I *should* tell you more, you're right." Helen paused. Sara could tell from her mother's voice that she was holding back tears. "Unfortunately, your father is not improving as quickly as we all had hoped. In fact, he's in the hospital right now for some tests."

"He's in the hospital?" Sara was startled. "But why? What's wrong with him?"

"Well, you remember when he was in Lexington Hospital going through 'cold turkey'?"

"I remember. It didn't help him."

"You're right, it didn't help him then. Those doctors didn't care enough. But now he's seeing doctors who do care. And now that he's not taking drugs again, he's gotten ill again with cramps and chills. The doctors here know what to do. And they think it's best to monitor him in the hospital."

"So that's why Daddy can't talk to me? Because he's in the hospital, but you didn't want to tell me? Are you telling me the truth *this* time?" Sara didn't know what she could believe anymore.

"Yes, Sara. I didn't want to trouble you, and I knew things would eventually be fine."

"You should have told me. I want you to tell me the truth." After a pause, she asked, "Will Daddy really get well this time?"

"Yes, sweetheart. Remember I told you not to worry. Hospitals did pull Daddy out of tough spots before. Before Daddy went to Lexington, he thought well of hospitals."

"What hospital was Daddy in before?"

"A hospital in England once saved Daddy's life."

"When was Daddy in England?"

"During the war. You remember. Daddy told you he was a World War II veteran."

Sara nodded.

"He was overseas in England and in France."

Sara had not given much thought to her father's service in the war. When he told her he didn't want to keep any war memories alive in his mind, she hadn't asked him any more about the war. But now she wanted to know more. "What did Daddy do in the war?"

"He enlisted in the Army Corps of Engineers shortly after we got married," her mother said slowly.

"Did he know about the concentration camps like Bergen-Belsen?"

"He knew about them, Sara. Afterward, like we all did. But he wasn't stationed near the camps. He saw fighting in France and got sent home after the big invasion in Normandy."

"He saw fighting!" She had to pause. *No wonder he doesn't want to remember.* "Why was he sent home?"

Her mother started coughing and couldn't stop.

"Are you OK, Ma?"

She finally stopped coughing. "Daddy got sick. He had chest pains, so we thought it was his heart. But it wasn't. He developed…a bad case of pleurisy and had to come home from the war. The telegram from the army hospital in England called it 'pulmonary disease.'"

"You have a telegram!" For a moment, Sara got excited thinking there was tangible proof of her father's service in the war. She imagined holding the piece of paper, touching it. She thought of showing the telegram to Ruth, to Miss Heller, and to the other students in her class. *My father was in the war and fought the Nazis! Maybe he could speak to my class.*

"Yes, sweetheart," Helen said. "I saved the telegram."

"I'd like to see it when you come home. And I want to talk to Daddy next time. Will you tell him hello for me? Tell him I miss him and want him to get better very soon."

"Of course, sweetie. You'll speak to him when he's home from the hospital."

But when Helen's next call came, her mother again apologized and said that her father wasn't available, even though he was finally out of the hospital. "I'm so sorry, Sara, but your Daddy, well, he can't talk right now."

"Why the heck not?" Sara yelled, intolerant of more excuses.

"Don't be fresh!" Helen said, but she caught herself, and hesitated. "Your father seems to have lost a lot of his memory."

"You're lying! I don't believe you anymore. You're hiding something from me. What is it?"

"There's nothing to hide, Sara," she responded. "You know we're in Florida so Daddy can get better. Well, now he's recuperating, not only from withdrawal, but from all the hospital tests, too. You can't imagine how much sleep he needs. Like a baby. He told me to tell you he loves you. Please understand, honey. I don't want to disturb him now."

"I don't believe you! Don't call me anymore!" Sara shouted, and then burst into tears. "I refuse to talk to you!" She turned the phone over to her aunt and said, "Tell Ma I won't talk to her until she and Daddy come home! It's been too long."

Visibly nervous, Annette took the phone and spoke to Helen for several minutes. When she finished, she told Sara with a sternness Sara was not used to hearing from her aunt, "You've got to do what I say. Take the phone! Your mother will not get off the line until you speak to her!"

Reluctantly Sara took the receiver back into her hand and shouted at her mother, "I don't want to hear any more of your lies."

"You won't hear any more lies," Helen said. "I'll tell you the whole truth."

"What's the 'truth' *now*?" Sara yelled. "I can't believe anything you say."

"Calm down, Sara. I was reluctant to tell you the truth because you get excited so easily. But you're insisting, so I'll tell you. Daddy and I need to be in Florida a bit longer because the doctors want to continue observing your father. Daddy trusts these doctors and wants them to help him. But in order for us to remain in Florida, we had to find part-time work. We don't want to keep taking money gifts from Grandma and Poppy. Our stay in Florida is getting much too expensive."

"What are you saying?" Sara blurted out. "How can Daddy work? I thought he was too sick to work. I thought you were supposed to be on vacation so he wouldn't *have* to work."

"I didn't want to worry you. I've been working as a salesgirl in a bakery. Now you know. And I'm calling you now, at night, because I'm not on my job. But your father can't talk to you at night because that's when he's been working. He's playing his harmonica in a band."

"What are you talking about?" Sara shouted at the top of her lungs. "Daddy is playing in a band? You're working in a bakery? Then you really *have* been lying to me. I thought so!" Sara broke into tears again. "How can I ever trust you again?"

"Don't cry, Sara. I was trying to protect you."

"But, but..." Sara sobbed, "if you have jobs, you could be down there much, much longer. Is your life down there, or up here with us? You, you...you don't care about us at all!" She was so disappointed and angry, she could hardly get her words out. She couldn't remember ever feeling so miserable.

"We don't *want* to stay here, you stubborn child. Your father's greatest desire is to return to you and Robbie and Rachel. The very fact that your father is making music is a good sign."

"Why should I believe you? You've been lying to me all along! Something else is going on that you won't say!"

The voice in her head returned. *Your father will never recover. He'll never return.*

Chapter Eleven | 1959–1961

When Sara turned twelve and a half, Aunt Annette and Uncle Nat began going out on Saturday nights to see shows at the Brooklyn Fox Theater. They paid Sara to babysit for her sister, brother, and cousin, but she couldn't control them. They'd shout and race up and down the long apartment hallway like it was an Olympic track, and they refused to go to bed on time. Because Sara often felt like a confused and helpless child herself, babysitting only reminded her of her own parents' absence.

She had a fantasy of saving enough babysitting money to hop onto a Greyhound bus and turn up at her parents' efficiency apartment in Coconut Grove. When she got there, she'd let them have it for all the disappointments and worry they'd caused her. But she'd also let them know how happy she was to be with them again. When Sara told Ruth about her fantasy, she asked Sara why her parents were gone so long. Sara didn't dare to share her father's secret with Ruth, so she couched their absence in pretense: Her father was trying out new job possibilities and dragging his feet.

One day, with great excitement, Sara showed Ruth all the money she had saved and the map she had drawn by hand detailing her itinerary. Ruth didn't think the trip was a good idea, but she was willing to accompany Sara on the subway one afternoon to buy the tickets at the Port Authority. At the last moment, Sara changed her mind. *Ruth was right after all,* Sara thought as she stood there, feeling very small amidst the noisy crowds at the Port Authority and imagining making the lengthy trip on her own. She was also frightened by what she saw at the bus terminal—the homeless men, mostly older Negro men, wearing torn shirts and pants and do-rags on their heads, asking for handouts, and slurring their words, like her father did when he was high on drugs. Ruth said to her, "Sara, let's go home," and they took the subway back to Williamsburg.

Sara sometimes forgot about her situation by writing stories and traveling in her imagination. She was inspired to write about girls her age in Mexico, Africa, and Australia after studying the stamp collection her cousin Ben shared with her brother Robbie. She began talking to her mother on the phone again and told her about all the stories she was writing and submitting as assignments in Miss Heller's English class. "And, Ma," she shouted into the receiver one night, "I'll be graduating from junior high a year sooner than I thought, because I made the Special Progress class."

"That's great, honey. Your father will be so proud of your accomplishments."

"Is Daddy playing in the band tonight?" Sara asked.

Helen took a while to answer.

"Well, is he?" Sara demanded, her anxiety returning.

"Yes, Sara. But he told me to tell you that we'll return home by next summer. Don't hold me to it, but that should be a whole year before you graduate. Meanwhile, I'm marking my calendar: Sara graduates, June 1961."

Sara counted her fingers. "That's still six months away."

Sara figured that if her parents kept their word, she finally would see them after a year and a half.

The winter months passed slowly for Sara. Even spring could not lighten her spirits. It was July before she finally experienced a glimmer of joy when she learned that her parents would be coming home. In preparation for their homecoming, Annette tidied up the apartment and prepared a meal in their honor with Sara's help. Annette even called and invited Sara's grandparents.

"Oh no, Mrs. Katz," Sara heard her aunt say. "Not diabetes! And you're not used to taking the insulin. It must be difficult. We'll miss you. Take care. I'll put Sara on."

"Hi, Grandma. Yes, Ma and Daddy will be here any day now. Thank you for your good wishes. I'm sorry you're not feeling well. I hope you feel better. Yes, I promise to tell Daddy you'll call. I hope we'll visit you soon."

On the evening before her parents' arrival, Sara couldn't sleep. She was too excited about seeing them and living with them again, this time with her father healed and healthy.

"Mommy and Daddy are here!" Rachel shouted the moment Helen and Josef walked in the door.

At last, Sara thought. She crossed her fingers behind her back, hoping her parents' extra-long stay in Florida achieved what they had hoped for—a cure for her father.

"Let me see you kids," Helen said, opening her arms. To Sara, her mother looked glamorous in white slacks and a bright yellow blouse that tied around her neck. Her voice had a honeyed sweetness.

Josef, in an open-necked floral shirt, quickly swept Rachel, Robbie, and Sara up in his arms before they could even reach Helen. "My wonderful children!" he said, hugging them tightly.

"Daddy, daddy!" Rachel shouted, squirming out of his grip. "Look what I have." She quickly ran into the kitchen and returned holding a kitten in her arms, a stray she had found that Annette allowed her to keep.

"Not now, sweetheart," her aunt said.

"It's OK," Josef said, ruffling Rachel's hair.

"What have you got there, sweetheart?" Helen said, smiling. "I see my Rachel loves animals."

"Do you want to pet Whiskers, Mommy?" Rachel handed her pet over to her mother, who took the kitten affectionately in her arms. She turned to Annette. "How can we ever thank you enough! My dear sister."

Annette blushed. "Don't mention it. We're family."

"Where's Nat?" Josef asked.

"He's painting a house on Bedford Avenue. He'll join us later."

Helen placed Whiskers on the floor, took out Panama hats from a large shopping bag, and placed them on the younger children's heads. Rachel scooped up her kitten and ran to the bedroom to look at herself in the mirror.

Sara was about to say, "What about me, Ma?" when her mother added, "For you, Miss Sara, we have this fine diary, with a cover made of mother of pearl." She squeezed Sara's hand.

"Oh, Mom!" Sara said, pleased and fascinated by the beautiful object.

"We know you've been writing," Josef said. Then he looked at Robbie, now ten and a half, and his cousin Ben, three years younger. "You boys been having a good time?"

"Yes, Uncle Josef," Ben said. Robbie simply stared at his father.

"Dad, did you forget?" Robbie said, looking worried. "Did you bring me the live shark tooth I asked for?"

Josef smiled. He pulled out a large, pointy tooth from his shirt pocket. "I didn't forget, son."

"Wow, Dad! Thanks."

"Are you and Ben collecting shark teeth because you're playing pirates?" Josef asked.

"Nope," Robbie said. "That's a good guess, but really I'm a scientist and Ben is my assistant. Come see what I've done." He pulled his father into the bathroom where his aunt and uncle had allowed him to set up a makeshift laboratory with bacteria growing in petri dishes and different-colored chemicals in test tubes. Ben followed them.

Meanwhile Sara fixed her gaze on her mother. She had always thought her mother was good-looking, but now she looked like a movie star with her bronzed complexion and shining teeth. Sara had always loved watching her apply her makeup. She'd darken her tweezed eyebrows with brown pencil using quick, short strokes. Then she'd apply eyeliner, silver-blue eye shadow, coral rouge, and rosy pink lipstick. Now, however, Helen's beauty appeared more natural, and Sara felt good seeing her mother so healthy looking. "Did you have a good time in Florida, Ma?"

Helen hesitated before answering. "Your father and I did what we had to do. We made the best of it. But honestly, sweetheart, we couldn't wait to be home, to return to you and your brother and sister."

For a fleeting second, Sara felt an impulse to say, "Then why did you stay away so long?" but being overjoyed with her mother and father's return, she refrained from any complaint that would mar the perfection of the moment.

The phone rang. It was Grandma Hannah, Annette announced, for Josef. Sara heard her father say cheerfully, after picking up the phone, "We're fine. Don't worry." Then he frowned. "You have diabetes. That's awful, Ma. How are you managing? You don't like injecting the insulin? Pop needs to help you? That's tough. We'll drive out to see you. Tomorrow. With the children. How's that? Good. Fine."

Helen spoke. "So sorry to hear about your mother, Josef. Will she be OK?"

He nodded. "She's adjusting. She'll be happy to see us and the kids."

"Sara," Helen continued, "Grandma will be surprised to see how grown-up you've become. Aunt Annette tells me you followed Grandma's recipe and baked us all a chocolate cake."

Sara smiled. "Yes, Ma. And I've been writing for my school newspaper and earning money babysitting."

"I'm very proud of you, sweetheart," Helen said.

Aunt Annette was beaming as she brought a bowl filled with colorful fruits to the table that Sara had set up in the living room for their buffet lunch. Sara rushed to move the other platters aside to make room for the fruit and for the chocolate cake she would soon bring out.

"Thanks for your help, Sara," Annette said, placing the paper goods and utensils on the table. "Helen, I can't pretend it's been ideal having all the children here with Nat and me. But it has been good. We've gotten to know your children better, and we're glad to do our part for the family."

"You and Nat have been saints," Helen responded. "Like parents to our kids. We know it hasn't been easy." Embracing her sister, she said, "We won't forget what you've done. We'll gather the children's things later this afternoon and move back to Penn Street. Honestly, I can't wait to set foot back in our apartment. Thank God Josef's parents kept the apartment for us."

Listening to her mother, Sara imagined how wonderful it would be to sleep once again in her own bed.

Once Sara's family settled back into their apartment on Penn Street, they returned to most of their previous routines, except that in the fall Robbie began attending Hebrew school in addition to public school, and Rachel was becoming a bit of a tomboy playing marbles and other street games with boys her age. On some weekends, Josef coached Robbie in Hebrew, took him out to Prospect Park to fly his kite, and taught Rachel how to roller skate and to ride a bicycle with training wheels. Sara continued making strides in middle school. Miss Heller recommended her for the editorial board of *The Rocket*, the school newspaper, and her writing covered the inauguration of John F. Kennedy, his establishment of the Peace Corps, and the protections he established for the Freedom Riders who were trying to integrate schools in the South.

Sara's mind was filled, however, with unanswered questions about her father. *If Daddy was fully better, then why wasn't he driving us to Queens most weekends to see Grandma and Poppy like he used to, especially now that Grandma suffered with diabetes? Didn't he want to take them out for rides in the Cadillac they gave him? And why did he still leave us on so many Saturdays to work in the city? What had really happened in Florida?*

For Sara, it all boiled down to understanding more fully, once and for all, the depth of her father's addiction, how it had started, and why it had stuck with him for so long. She was tempted many times to approach her father with her questions, but she didn't want him to think she doubted his recovery. Better to ask her mother, Sara thought, especially since her mother had promised many times to tell her about her father's past. Sara thought of herself as being mature enough now to hear about her father's history. But each time Sara raised these questions with her mother, Helen's face turned downcast, and she'd say she wasn't ready to talk. Helen still didn't believe the time was right to discuss these matters with Sara.

Her mother's unwillingness to talk frustrated Sara, and her old anger against her mother began to brew. *I need to know,* Sara thought even more persistently. *Why does Ma feel the need to keep secrets from me?*

The plans for Sara's graduation party kept Sara's mind off these troubling questions. The party would be held in a special room in the synagogue rented out for family events. Rabbi Korn told Sara's mother he was pleased that in time Robbie's *bar mitzvah* party would be held there, too. His Conservative congregation of Russian Jewish immigrants was dwindling, so he was especially happy when families celebrated their joyous events, their *simchas,* in the synagogue and his services were fully attended, as they had been decades ago. Now the only synagogues in Williamsburg that were growing were those attended by the ultra-Orthodox who believed literally in the coming of the Messiah and were waiting for his arrival. Their children went to their own schools and didn't mix with Conservative Jewish children.

The party room was large enough to hold a dinner and have musicians play live music that people could dance to, so Josef planned to play his harmonica as well as cater the party with delicatessen treats from Katz and Block Kosher Meats. With her mother's help, Sara designed the guest list that included their close relatives and Sara's friends from the neighborhood and her school. Of course, Uncle Nat, Aunt Annette, and Cousin Ben would be present. So would Grandma and Poppy. There would also be Daddy's partner, Uncle Irv, and Daddy's sister, Aunt Rozzie, and their two children, Sara's cousins, all of whom lived in Queens. Sara's friend Ruth would be invited, along with Ruth's mother and two brothers, and a group of teenagers from Middle School 318—some writers from the school newspaper and others who were Sara's classmates. Sara and Ruth had fun thinking of who would be dancing with whom to the records they'd be playing: "The Twist," "I'm Sorry," "Runaway," and "Shop Around." And when Robbie listened to "Runaround Sue" on the Victrola, he insisted that

Sara teach him how to do the Lindy. He wanted to have a whirl on the dance floor at the party, too.

On the Saturday of the graduation party, Josef surprised the family by saying he had business to do in Manhattan that afternoon.

"No, Daddy, not today!" Sara shouted, her heart sinking.

"Your business will have to wait," Helen insisted. "Where is your sense of priority?"

"I wish my appointment could wait," Josef said kindly but firmly, "but it can't. I'm very sorry. But don't worry, I've arranged for all the deli platters to be delivered to the party room in plenty of time for the gathering."

"But it's you, Daddy, that I want to be with us!" Sara protested.

When Helen complained over the phone to Josef's sister Rozzie about these Saturday appointments, Uncle Irv got on the phone. He confirmed that Josef had to meet with certain deli owners who were their customers, reminding Helen that Josef was much better at personal relations than he was. Uncle Irv apologized for the poor timing of these meetings, but he told Helen that they would not extend into the evening; he assured Helen that Josef could definitely be home for the party.

Sara was worried that her father would not personally be present to help with the setup. There were streamers to be hung, tables and chairs to be arranged, the new stereo that Grandma and Poppy bought for Sara to be hooked up, along with a special microphone for Josef's harmonica playing and the tributes that family members and friends were going to present.

Everything had to be done quickly after the Sabbath ended, so several helping hands were needed. Josef gave Robbie a pep talk before he left for Manhattan after breakfast, telling him to help his mother and sister with lifting anything heavy if by some chance he was late. Sara said she would ask Mrs. Taylor if her sons could help. Josef said he'd feel better if another adult were also there, so he engaged one of the synagogue maintenance staff to meet Helen at the party room when they began to set up.

"Helen, smile," he said. "It will work out fine." He gave Sara a kiss on her forehead and said, "See you a little later, Sha-Sha."

The deli platters arrived at 7:30 p.m. By that time, Sara, her mother and Robbie, Ruth Taylor and her brothers, and Herb, the maintenance man, had set everything up. The room looked lovely with several round tables, a wooden platform for dancing, and dimmed lights like those in a nightclub. Sara wore one of her favorite pleated skirts so she could dance easily, and she kept her brown hair loose, with a headband to keep strands out of her eyes. Because Sara was now fourteen, Helen allowed her to wear some light eye makeup and lipstick.

Guests began to arrive at 8 p.m.—Aunt Annette with her family, Rachel and Whiskers, then Mrs. Taylor and all of Sara's friends. Rachel promised to hold onto Whiskers. The guests congratulated Sara, placed their gifts on a special card table, and mingled with one another happily as they found seats for themselves. Sara's friends began to dance to the records on the stereo. Then Uncle Irv arrived from Queens with Aunt Rozzie, Sara's cousins, and Grandma and Poppy. Grandma Hannah kissed Sara on the cheek as she placed a chocolate cake baked in Sara's honor on the buffet table. Helen nervously invited all the guests to enjoy the dinner, disturbed that Josef had still not appeared.

"Where's Josef?" Grandma Hannah asked Helen. "I haven't seen him in weeks!"

"I was going to ask Irv the same thing," Helen said. "He didn't call me to say he'd be late. But then again, I've been down here without a phone for hours. I thought he might have called you."

"No, Helen," Irv said. "Not a word from him. I'd better call the New Yorker Deli. That was his last stop."

"Call now," Grandma Hannah insisted. "There's a phone in the office. Is the door open, Helen?"

"Yes, Ma. Please, Irv. Call now!"

By 8:30 p.m. Josef had not arrived, though Irv learned he had left his last deli stop a couple of hours before. Sara was deeply hurt and confused by her father's absence. *Where was he? Was he just late, caught in some terrible traffic jam? Or was it something more serious?*

Her heart heavy with disappointment and fear, Sara could not enjoy the party. She sensed the discomfort of her friends who, as they ate, were whispering at their tables. She imagined they were too polite to ask where her father was, since she had boasted to them they would hear him play the harmonica. This was certainly not the party Sara had imagined.

Helen, frantic by this turn of events, said goodbye to her guests at 9:30 p.m., promising Grandma and Poppy she would let them know about Josef's whereabouts as soon as she knew anything. Irv agreed to call Helen as soon as he dropped his family back home in Queens. If he had to, he'd drive back to Brooklyn to help Helen.

"No need for you to do that, Irv," Uncle Nat said. "I live around the corner. I can help Helen."

The voice in Sara's head sounded grim: *Something terrible has happened to your father.*

Chapter Twelve | 1961–1963

After Sara's graduation party, Helen and the children returned to their apartment. Shortly afterward Helen received a phone call. She spoke to the caller in such subdued tones that Sara was unable to hear her mother's words.

"Was that Daddy?" Rachel asked.

Sara thought it might be her father but did not ask.

"Yes, honey. Daddy's on his way home."

Sara could hear the hesitancy in her mother's voice and sensed how upset she was. "It's too late to wait up for Daddy, children. You've had a fun evening with your big sister—lots of excitement—and now it's time to rest. You'll see Daddy in the morning. Go on now, get ready for bed."

"Do we have to?" Robbie said, pouting.

"Yes, sir," Helen said. She closed their bedroom door once they got into their pajamas.

When Helen and Sara were alone in the kitchen, Helen could no longer control herself and began to cry. She told Sara it was the police who had called. Josef had crashed into a street lamp after driving his van over the Williamsburg Bridge. "He's not injured," Helen quickly added, trembling. "I'm so relieved."

"Ma, how terrible!" Sara said, hugging her mother. "You're sure he's OK? How did it happen?"

"I don't know. I don't know. The police will be here with Daddy any minute. I'm afraid he'll be arrested."

"Arrested? Why? For having an accident?"

Her mother stared at Sara without answering.

The doorbell rang, and when she opened the door, Helen faced a tall, sandy-haired officer who was holding Josef's arm. "Officer Kelly, ma'am. Mrs. Katz, your husband has lost his license."

"Yes, officer," Helen said meekly. She looked at Josef, whose eyes were half-closed.

Officer Kelly handed Helen a copy of his written report and escorted Josef, who was groggy and unsteady on his feet, into the foyer. "Your husband is in shock. He fell asleep at the wheel. A medic checked him out, and he seems fine, but you'll want a doctor to examine him in the morning."

"Oh no," Helen gasped. "Asleep at the wheel! Thank God he's alive." She reached for Josef's hand.

Josef lifted his head and opened his eyes. They were clouded over with what looked like a gauzy, yellow film. "I…I'ze sorry, Helen. I…I…tried…"

Sara, standing by her mother's side, felt thankful that her father was alive, but his sorry condition startled her. He was slurring his words the same way he had the night he got high on heroin and lost the tip of his finger in the swinging kitchen door. *Did he really fall asleep while he was driving? Or was it something much worse?*

"The paperwork explains what you have to do," the officer continued. "You'll need to come to the precinct tomorrow."

"The precinct?" Helen's voice was tense. "I never…"

"I know where it is, Ma." Officer Kelly looked at Sara.

"This is our daughter, sir," Helen said.

"Good evening, young lady." The policeman looked around. "Throwing a party?" From the foyer, he could see party trays of leftover food, cake, and soda on the kitchen counter.

Josef spoke up again. "My daughter's graj-u-a-shun. Top A...student."

The officer turned his gaze on Helen, who was still holding onto Josef's hand. "We celebrated our daughter's graduation this evening, Officer Kelly," she said, tears rolling down her cheek. "My husband didn't show up, and I was so worried."

Officer Kelly read aloud from his copy of the report. "'Katz and Block *Kosher* Meat, Williamsburg.' If you're *kosher*—please pardon my ignorance—how come you people aren't wearing dark clothes like the other Jewish people I see in this neighborhood?"

"We're not Orthodox," Sara said.

"Uh-huh. You're Jewish but not Orthodox?"

"That's right," Helen answered nervously, as if she were afraid that Officer Kelly was somehow casting suspicion on who they were. She held onto Sara more tightly.

Officer Kelly looked at the three of them huddled together. To Josef he said, "I see you have a caring family. You almost lost your life tonight. When—or if—you get your license back, save those Manhattan kosher meat deliveries until you've had enough sleep. I don't want to have to see you again, Mr. Katz—you hear me?"

"Yessir," Josef said, bobbing his head up and down.

When the officer left, Helen helped Josef into the bedroom and encouraged him to lie down and go to sleep. Sara was pacing in the kitchen when Helen returned.

"Is Daddy on drugs again, Ma?"

"I'm sorry, Sara. Daddy doesn't want me discussing his condition. Before we returned from Florida, we agreed not to say anything about Daddy's problem to the family, not even to Grandma and Poppy. Anyway, this is supposed to be a happy time for you."

"How can I be happy? Daddy's still sick—and you're still keeping secrets from me!"

"Your father thinks you know too much already."

"He does not! I don't believe you! Tell me why you thought Daddy would be arrested. I need to know."

"Sit down, Sara." A sober expression appeared on her face. "I'll tell you. I don't want you to worry." She began slowly. "I'm sad to say…your father is still on drugs. What happened in Florida wasn't good like we had hoped." She took a deep breath. "I'll start with the hospital. They kept him there as long as they could, but he left against the doctor's orders. He never finished the cold turkey treatment. And he went downhill after he left. He still craved heroin, as much as ever."

"Oh, Mom, how awful! After all Daddy went through. After all you've been through." Crushed with disappointment, Sara could hardly get the words out.

"Before he joined the band, he'd hunt up and down Collins Avenue and Miami Beach, looking for a fix, looking for a pusher."

Sara listened in stunned disbelief.

Helen continued, "When he left our efficiency apartment, I followed him, in the dark, to the beach. Most times, he couldn't find drugs or couldn't afford what he found. So instead he'd get drunk on vodka, scotch, or beer—or he took different kinds of medications, anything to quiet his symptoms." Her voice had become shrill. She shook her head back and forth. "We'd drag ourselves back to our apartment and your father would drop off to sleep in a stupor, like he did tonight. Who knows what he's on now!"

Her mother's words were too much for Sara, too maddening. All this time she had been waiting for her parents' return, expecting to see her father well, her mother less burdened. Could this really be happening? "Tell me it's not true, Ma. I don't want it to be true!"

"I wish it were a bad dream," she said, closing her heavy-lidded eyes.

"What about the job Daddy had—the band he played in with his harmonica?"

"He did play at the Stardust Hotel. But it turned out..." She hesitated, took a cigarette from her pocket, put it to her lips, and fumbled with the match. "It turned out that many of the band members were addicts, and pushers hung out there, too."

Sara's stomach dropped. Helen closed her eyes and began to cry again. "I tried to stop your father from shooting up."

"Stop him? How?" Sara's mind flashed with terror to that night six and a half years ago, when her mother had tried before to stop her father. That time he pushed her and hit her, and she wound up sprawled on the floor.

"I was trying to help him," Helen said weakly.

"How were you helping him, Mom? You're talking in circles and making me nervous. What does all of this have to do with Daddy being arrested?"

Helen groaned. "No one knows. I promised your father..."

Sara abruptly rose from her chair. "Mom, please stop with the secrets. Not knowing is making me crazy!"

"All right, *mamela.* Maybe it's better if it comes out. I was afraid there would be a raid at the hotel, and if your father was caught with heroin, he'd be arrested and sent to prison. So I went to the Stardust with him, thinking that would keep him out of trouble. But I couldn't stop him. And the pushers took me for a junkie, too. I couldn't do anything to stop your father. I was terrified...because...your father...had been caught with heroin and arrested before."

"Oh no! What happened to him?"

"He wouldn't give the police the names they wanted. They wanted him to tell them who the pushers were. But he wouldn't do it, so he was in jail for eight months. That's why he couldn't ever talk to you on the phone. He was in jail! That's the real reason why we had to stay in Florida so long. Oh, *mamela,* I'm so sorry."

Sara sat speechless, not knowing what to think. Her feelings were in utter chaos.

Helen continued. "Everything we hoped for in Florida boomeranged. Your father's still addicted, and I'm...I'm more mixed up and desperate than ever."

"What's wrong with Daddy? Other addicts recover. Why can't he?"

Her mother turned her head away. Finally she said, "I've been telling your father about a doctor in Harlem I read about who has had success with methadone. But he won't listen to me. He thinks he'd only be substituting one addiction for another."

Sara didn't expect such a response. Hadn't her mother rejected methadone, too, for the same reason? "You mean he'll always be an addict?"

"He'd probably be less sick with methadone. He could get the treatment legally. And he might be able to get off of it… eventually."

Sara took this information in. Her father was in such deep trouble, he couldn't ever get out of it without big consequences. *Oh why did he turn to heroin in the first place? Did he know it would ruin his life?*

"So you think Daddy's unwilling to try methadone because there are no guarantees?"

"When the right time comes, *mamela*, you'll understand how difficult his situation is."

In the days that followed, Josef couldn't drive into Manhattan because his drivers' license had been revoked. Instead he worked in the neighborhood with Uncle Irv in their retail shop. Sometimes, when Sara returned home from school, he'd be at home, feeling sick. Sara heard her mother one afternoon pleading with him to try methadone.

"There's a chance, Josef, that you could feel better. You could get your license back and make your wholesale deliveries."

"Forget it, Helen. I'm sick of *chances*. Those clinics are just rackets to stop junkies from roaming the streets. There's no benefit to me."

"The benefit is not having to suffer with your symptoms. Look at you, shivering with chills! You've been through withdrawal before. You could reduce your pain."

"What about the mental pain I'd have at a clinic? The humiliation?"

The arguments continued. When Sara overheard them shouting at each other at night, she couldn't sleep. She began thinking about courageous women in conflict with their husbands who found ways to leave their marriages.

On some nights, Sara would quietly turn on the lamp beside her bed, careful not to wake her brother or sister. She'd take out the mother-of-pearl diary her parents brought her from Florida and jot down notes for her stories. In the morning, she would elaborate on the scenes using characters and dialogue from her imagination. Once she was finished revising these stories, she submitted them to her new English teacher at Eastern District High School, Miss Newman, who encouraged her to collect her writings in a special folder, telling her they might be useful when she applied to college.

When Miss Newman instructed Sara to explore different themes, Sara chose to write about Miss Newman herself and her other teachers, single women in their forties, and their struggles to make careers for themselves. Sara also wanted to write a story about her friend Ruth's mother, another woman on her own, whose life was even more complicated because she had children.

Sara was still curious about why Ruth's father had abandoned his family, but she realized that in order for her to talk about him to Ruth, she'd have to be ready to share information about her own father, and this made her hesitate. Also, she didn't have her father's whole story, his history as a heroin addict.

When Eleanor Roosevelt died in November 1962, Miss Newman asked Sara to write a memorial tribute for *Legacy*, Eastern District's literary magazine. Sara was happy to write the article and focused it on how prominent Mrs. Roosevelt had been as First Lady during Franklin Roosevelt's administration and how her importance continued internationally after the president's death. Writing the article called to mind Miss Heller's class on famous people with handicaps, which was when she first learned about Mrs. Roosevelt's childhood. It occurred to Sara that there were some similarities between Mrs. Roosevelt's childhood and her own.

Mrs. Roosevelt had become an orphan when she was ten years old. That was Sara's age when her father went into Hawthorne Lodge for shock therapy. Mrs. Roosevelt's father was an alcoholic who had been banished from the family. Sara wondered how alcoholism differed from her father's addiction to heroin, and she wondered if banishing her father might have been better for her family. Why had her mother been so devoted to her father despite the years of pain he caused her? Why was she so tolerant?

On some mornings, usually after Sara's parents had been arguing at night, Josef didn't get up for work and simply stayed in bed. Observing this, Sara wrote in her diary, "Addiction is such a powerful sickness—it robs a person of the desire to work and even to live." With Josef working less and less, her mother realized that to make ends meet, she'd need to work. She'd been a wife and mother her entire married life and hadn't even graduated from high school, but she found a job with Field's Department Store in downtown Brooklyn doing market research. Sara, in the days following, became her brother and sister's babysitter after school, watched her father become sicker and sicker, and heard her mother's continued urgings that her father go to a methadone clinic.

A question popped into Sara's head after dinner one night as she dried the dishes. Once her father had gone to bed, she couldn't keep quiet. "Mom, why have you stayed married to Daddy? Why didn't you leave him?"

Her mother turned the faucet off and took the dish towel from Sara. She stood by the sink, drying her hands and looking at Sara in shock.

"That man in the bedroom, who's worked as hard as he possibly could to stop his addiction and who's now fighting to save his life—you want to know why I haven't left him?"

Sara felt ashamed. And yet she wondered: Had her father really worked as hard as her mother said to stop his addiction? Did her mother really believe that, or did her feelings change from day to day? Hadn't her mother's arguments with her father been much more frequent lately? She must at times have thought her life could be easier without him.

"Your father's a suffering human being," Helen continued. "I've seen his pain up close these past years, and I could never desert him."

Could Sara possibly think of her father the way her mother was now describing him? Was he a heroic victim honestly trying to survive his illness, trying again and again to beat it by going cold turkey? She wasn't convinced. "If you think Daddy's trying so hard, why are you angry at him for not going to a methadone clinic?"

"Because...because...I'm afraid we could lose him!"

Sara's fears revived that her father was dying, but they subsided now and then when he had a good day. On those days he would help Robbie with science projects for school or with the Hebrew Robbie needed for his *bar mitzvah*. Or he would take Rachel across Broadway to the Lorimer Street playground where he'd push her on the swings.

Sara wondered if it was time for that long-overdue talk she had always meant to have with him. She could hear herself telling him, "Daddy, I need you to get well—the whole family does. I should have spoken to you long, long ago. I'm so sorry I didn't. There has to be an answer for you. Other people with your problem have gotten well. You can, too. I know you can, Daddy. Please try the methadone Mom has heard about. Maybe it will work. I love you so much—what can I do to help you?"

Would she have the courage to speak these words? Would he hear her?

Chapter Thirteen | 1963

One morning when Sara's father was feeling too sick to leave for work, she heard him shouting to her mother from the bedroom. "Helen, I've told you so many times. Those clinics are hopeless. Drop the subject! A Jew like me can't be helped in places where misguided ministers just want us to sing 'Amazing Grace.'"

Lingering to hear them argue made Sara late for school that morning.

She feared time was running out, and she still hadn't found a way to speak to her father. What if he died from his addiction and she hadn't ever tried to save him with her words?

That evening, after hearing Walter Cronkite on the news, her mother ran into the kitchen where Josef sat brooding.

"Josef!" Sara heard her yell. "He's on TV—Dr. Barish! The one I've been reading about. His clinic in East Harlem is getting results with methadone! I could kick myself for throwing those newspapers out."

Her father simply grunted. "Methadone won't stop my craving."

"But the articles I've read say it can," she insisted.

Sara heard the frustration in her mother's voice. Sara, too, wanted to convince her father to give the clinic a chance. She thought if she had real proof of Dr. Barish's success, she might be able to convince her father. She considered taking the subway to Harlem by herself, but she realized that even if she could find the clinic, speak to Dr. Barish, and see firsthand the treatment he offered, her words alone would not hold much weight with her father—and it would upset her mother. And she couldn't ask her friend Ruth to travel with her, because Ruth still didn't know about her father's problem, and Helen had sworn Sara to secrecy about it. If only she could find the newspaper articles about Dr. Barish that her mother had read, she could show them to her father. That would give her words more power. She would try her best this time not to get intimidated and tongue-tied when she faced him.

That Sunday, instead of doing her school work at home, she rode the bus from downtown Brooklyn up Flatbush Avenue to the Grand Army Plaza Library, to be there when it opened at 1 p.m. She felt confident that one of the librarians would help her find the information about Dr. Barish that she needed so badly. Maybe she would find Miss Schwartz, who had assisted her in the past to find material for the articles she wrote for Eastern District's literary journal.

How fortunate that Miss Schwartz was seated at her desk in the large reading room! Seeing Sara, she smiled warmly. "Miss Katz," she exclaimed, "I've been saving something for you!" She placed a folder in front of Sara. "Mexico's foremost female naturalist just sent her unique butterfly stamp series to the library. It occurred to me you might be interested in writing about her and her collection in your column."

"Thank you so much for thinking of me, Miss Schwartz. But...I wonder if you could...I would appreciate your help so much..." Sara had difficulty framing her request.

"What is it, dear?"

"I need to find out...about...about..." Finally, she got the words out. "A methadone clinic that's been in the news."

"A methadone clinic?"

Sara nodded. Miss Schwartz adjusted her glasses squarely on her nose. "Do you have a name for the clinic, a location?"

In a flash, Sara produced some notes she had jotted down and placed them nervously on Miss Schwartz's desk.

"Barish? Dr. Barish?" she repeated, thumbing through the clippings in some folders on the desk. "I remember reading something about him," she mused. But her folders didn't yield what she was looking for, so she rose from her chair and continued her search in the stacks.

At last, she found two items: a photo of Dr. Barish taken at his recent appearance on *The Tonight Show* with Johnny Carson and an article in *The New York Times*. The photo showed a Nordic-looking man: fair, tall, and well-built. The title of the article read, "Doctor Has Hope for Heroin Addicts."

The article cheered Sara greatly. She sat reading at a long wooden table, her legs crossed at the ankles, streams of sunlight brightening the room. The author of the article praised Mayor Wagner for the storefront clinics he endorsed in all the boroughs. The research at Columbia University and Rockefeller Hospital showed that methadone could be an effective treatment when combined with adequate counseling. The article then mentioned the dark days of World War II, when addiction among fear-ridden troops was kept top-secret by the military. Reading this, Sara became alarmed. Her mother had said that her father's addiction began before they got married, before her father served in the war. Was it possible his addiction continued even during his military service? Her mother had saved her father's discharge papers from 1944, along with a telegram informing her that Josef would be returning home with "pulmonary disease."

Sara remembered that Helen had also kept two copies of an article from *The Daily Mirror* that included photos of Josef's landing at Mitchel Field in a four-motored C-54 Air Transport Command hospital plane with other soldiers who had crashed at Normandy and were hit hard by the enemy.

Was "pulmonary disease" a way of hiding the truth? Sara wondered. She had never bothered to investigate the codes on her father's discharge notice—"CDD" and "AW 107." But now she suddenly wondered, *What was the* real *cause of her father's discharge?* She decided she would do the research as soon as her family crisis was over.

As she read on, her fears increased. She learned that New York City's problem with heroin addiction had reached epidemic proportions. Between 1950 and 1961, fatalities related to heroin injections had become the leading cause of young adult deaths in the city. And the situation now, a year later, was getting worse due to a growing influx of smuggled heroin, cheaper and more pure, from Mexico, not from Turkey as before. "Drug-related crimes, deaths, and suicides," she read, "are becoming more and more rampant."

Without realizing it, Sara blurted out, "Oh no!" Miss Schwartz rushed over to where Sara was seated.

"Miss Katz, what's wrong?"

Sara turned white as a blank page. "Please forgive me, Miss Schwartz." Trying to calm herself, she said, "May I make copies of this material? I need to leave immediately."

Miss Schwartz pointed to a machine near the card catalogues. "Our brand new copier gives change."

Sara wished she could fly back home to Penn Street over the Sunday traffic, like she sometimes did in her dreams. She wanted her father, now in the throes of involuntary heroin withdrawal, to know that if he dared to pick up a bag of heroin on the street at this time, the statistics indicated that his chance of death was sky high.

She wanted to tell him what she had been trying to say to him since she was eight years old. If he no longer had the desire to live for himself, could he at least live for her, her mother, brother, and sister? That's what she would plead with him to do. Because they needed him. Because they loved him. Methadone might be a way out for him. She had to communicate this information immediately. As soon as she got home.

When she arrived home, her father was not in sight, and her mother, who was preparing dinner, was not alone.

"Hi, Grandma; hi, Poppy," Sara said. "Are you joining us for supper?"

They shook their heads no, but they didn't speak. Grandma Hannah was folding and unfolding her hands on the table. Poppy Mo was poring over pages in two of his ledgers, one that tracked the business he did each week in his Bedford Street butcher shop, the other that listed his tenants' monthly rent payments that Josef collected for him. In spite of his illness, Josef was still collecting his father's rents, even though he himself couldn't pay the rent he owed his parents for the apartment his family lived in. Helen's part-time salary barely kept the family going. A tense gloom hung in the air. Outside the street lamps on Penn Street had just come on.

Sara wanted to tell her mother what she had found out at the library, but she felt uncomfortable discussing this information in front of her grandparents.

"Where is everyone?" she asked, trying to sound casual.

In a shaky voice, Helen said, "Your father is lying down in the bedroom with the chills. Robbie is over at cousin Ben's, and Rachel is still playing marbles in the street with Ritchie. Didn't you see her when you walked into the building?"

There was a strange lull, and then Hannah said, "Sara, darling, I'm sorry to tell you your mother isn't talking to us. I guess she's angry."

Sara glanced at her mother, then at her grandmother. "Angry? Why?" She looked back and forth between her mother and grandparents.

Finally Hannah announced, "She's angry because Poppy and me decided your father should move in with us."

Sara didn't think she heard her grandmother correctly. "What did you say, Grandma?"

"I said," Hannah repeated, "that your mother is angry with us because we believe your father should live with us. We won't hide from you, Sara dear, what we think. We know you're aware of your father's problem. You're a grown girl of sixteen."

"You mean Daddy should leave *our* family to live with you?" Sara was bewildered by what she heard.

"Yes, *mamela*. Soon your father will get his driver's license back. You know what he'll do. He'll drive into the city to buy drugs, get high, and get into another accident. But if he's living with Poppy and me, we'll stop him."

The blood drained from Sara's face. "No, Grandma!" she screamed uncontrollably. "Please don't take my father away! It's crazy. You won't stop him by holding him hostage. Don't you understand? He needs a cure."

Before Hannah could answer, Helen turned from the stove and shouted, "You can't remove an adult man from his family as if he were a child! What's wrong with you? Are you insane?" She lunged toward them, waving her mixing spoon. Grandma Hannah and Poppy Mo flinched, as though they were afraid of being struck by Helen's spoon.

"But listen, Helen," Grandma said, defending herself. "Being around you and the kids, Josef takes you all for granted. He thinks no matter what he does, you'll accept it. He thinks he'll always have you."

Poppy, who allowed his wife to do all of the talking, shook his head in agreement.

"No, you're wrong, Grandma!" Sara said, still shouting. "Daddy doesn't take us for granted. He loves us, and you're not going to take him from us!"

"Don't you get it?" Helen yelled. "He's going cold turkey, weaning himself off heroin. He's not on drugs anymore, and he's not going to get them."

"That's just what you said when we sent you to Florida for a cure," Hannah cried, rising from her chair and standing behind Poppy. "But he found heroin there, didn't he? And he came back even sicker. That's why he's flat on his back, no good to anyone." She shook her head. "It will be hard, but we need to take him *away* from his family. If he knows that the only way he'll get you back is to stop taking heroin, maybe what he has to do will finally sink in."

With tears flowing down her cheeks, Sara looked at her grandparents and said pleadingly, "Grandma, Poppy…my father needs us. He can't move. We're keeping him alive. My mother found out about a new clinic. A methadone clinic. *The New York Times* praised it. I read about it in the library today!" She pulled the copies she'd made out of her book bag.

"*Vos is dos?* What is this? Methadone?" her grandfather said.

"You see, Poppy," Sara cried, "you and Grandma *don't* know what Daddy needs—not like my mother does!"

"We certainly know what your father needs, *sheyna maidel*," Grandma said. "If he needs a clinic, Poppy and me will take him there. Your mother's working, remember? She doesn't have the time."

"Don't you understand?" Helen shouted. "The children need their father! Robbie's *bar mitzvah* is right around the corner. He needs a loving father to teach him and coach him. And Rachel—she hardly knows who her father is, he's been in bed so long."

"Do you think we are happy about doing this?" Hannah asked. "We're broken people. I'm sick with diabetes. But we can't just watch Josef get worse. We've tried everything. Now it's up to us—we will watch him night and day, like hawks."

"But Grandma," Sara said, her chest tightening. "How can you possibly watch Daddy constantly? You work in the butcher shop."

"Not no more," Poppy Mo said. "The shop don't need for your grandmother to be there. She can pass out any minute if her sugar drops too low. Besides," he pointed to his ledger, "we're not making no money to stay open every day." He stood up beside Hannah and put his arm around her. "We can manage. We still got rents from the apartment building. So you see—your grandmother will take care of Josef."

Helen slammed her spoon on the counter in anger. "Have you asked your forty-two-year-old son how he feels leaving his family and living under his mother's roof like a baby? You think shaming and humiliating him will help him get better? I can't believe you think that having a grown man, a father of three children, live with you can possibly be of help to him!"

"He knows already about it," Hannah said. "We told him last week. He didn't like it, but he's going to do it."

"How could you possibly convince Daddy to leave us?" Sara asked.

"We have our ways," Hannah said, looking down, then up at Poppy.

"You're playing games with your son?" Helen screamed. "A sick man!"

Sara wanted her mother and grandmother to stop arguing. She wanted to speak to her father now, tell him about the danger he was in and talk about the methadone clinic where he could be treated. She wanted to make up for all the times she intended to talk to him and could not. She was about to plead with her grandparents not to go through with their plan, when Rachel walked in the door, her blonde hair sweaty, her overalls caked with dirt from the sidewalks. "Let me clean you up," Helen said, taking her arm.

"Our decision is made," Hannah said, ignoring Rachel and pulling on Mo's sleeve, motioning for them to go. "We'll get

Josef." They walked to his bedroom.

Sara was too upset for words.

Her mother shouted at them, "He's not well! Do you want to add punishment to his illness?" Her potatoes began boiling over. She rushed to turn the flame down. "He won't go with you. He won't leave us!" she shouted. Sara had never, ever seen her mother so distraught.

"He'll come!" Hannah said in a determined voice.

Sara couldn't believe these were the grandparents she knew. *How can they love us if they take our father away and make him follow them like a puppet? It feels like we're not part of the same family anymore. Should I try to talk to him right now, tell him what I learned about methadone, and stop him from leaving?* As these thoughts raced through her mind, she saw her father and grandparents walking from the bedroom, past the kitchen, and out the door of the apartment without saying anything.

"Josef!" Helen let out a scream. "Stop! You're not leaving!" She was holding Rachel in front of her as proof that their youngest child needed him.

Sara saw her little sister's confusion and bewilderment. She saw her father dressed in his gray silk suit. *Was it to make a good appearance to the neighbors?* His cheeks were red. Josef looked at Helen, at Sara, at Rachel. "I can't help it," he said. "If I don't go with them now..." He paused and took a deep breath. "If I don't go, they won't let you keep this apartment. We'll all be on the street." His body seemed to fold in defeat.

Sara's anger at her grandparents could have filled a room twice the size of the kitchen she stood in. She held onto her mother and sister. How could she ever have loved her grandparents? This must all be a bad dream.

On her way out of the apartment, Hannah said, "Don't worry about money, Helen. We'll cover your rent. You'll have all the eggs and poultry you need, all the meat you need. Josef will visit you and bring you everything."

Helen screamed at the top of her lungs, "Who needs your food, you stone-hearted bastards!"

Sara couldn't believe she was losing her father like this. "Daddy," she pleaded, seeking his eyes, "when will you be back?" But he didn't answer. "Daddy, stop!"

Sara would never forget the sight of him holding his suitcase, his face flushed, his pain visible in every feature.

The Lost Father

Chapter Fourteen | 1963

After the funeral of her father, and the *shiva,* the Jewish mourning period, Sara had been too upset to complete the homework Mr. Carney, her history teacher, had required. She was hoping he would excuse her from submitting the report, given the circumstances.

A few days after she returned to class, Mr. Carney said in a tone that was stern, but not without a hint of kindness, "Miss Katz, your make-up assignment is due today: How Did Roosevelt Lead the U.S. into World War II?"

Sara panicked. She didn't have it.

He knows I just lost my father. She ticked the time markers off on her fingers—two weeks ago, the funeral; then the week of *shiva*; then coming back to class. *He knows I'm a serious student, vice president of the General Organization. Another teacher might make an allowance.*

She squirmed in her seat.

"Johnny Rigo! Anthony Spinelli! Salvatore Carmen!" Mr. Carney shot the names of the delinquents out like rivets. "Big...fat...zeros...*lads,*" he enunciated slowly with his brogue. "*Ev'rythin's* overdue—from World War I to Sacco and Vanzetti."

The atmosphere in American History, suddenly still, frightened Sara. She wondered how she ever got placed in such a rough class. She turned her head from the front of the room, where the good students sat, to the rear, where the rocky boys were already half-standing, smirking, their leather jackets on.

"In your seats!" Carney demanded, peering down the aisle. "Jackets off! Class hasn't ended yet!"

In slow motion, the boys began rolling their jackets off their sleeves. Sara was fascinated by their indifference to school. Didn't they want to have jobs one day? To be somebody? On the wall, the big hand of the round-faced clock inched toward two-thirty. Friday afternoon, the week before Christmas. She heard the other students zipping up their pencil cases, gathering their books.

"Give him your fucking assignment, Sara," Johnny Rigo shouted from the rear.

Mr. Carney snapped back, "Enough out of you, Rigo! I'm suspending you again."

The boy, still grinning, strutted past Sara's desk. Sara stood up and told Mr. Carney quietly she didn't have the essay. She'd have it for him on Monday. He stared at her, his face stiff with annoyance. Then he barked at the class, "Dismissed."

On her way to pick up her younger siblings from school, Sara watched carefully for patches of ice on the sidewalks, berating herself because she hadn't done the assignment. *Only five pages to write. Reread the chapter. Do the research. It hasn't been hard in the past. So why...?* She saw the heavy weekend traffic lurch forward through the slush on Wilson Street as she waited for the red light. Her mind kept whizzing. *Am I still too furious at Daddy for dying?* Rachel and Robbie waved at her from a distance. *Am I still too angry at him for lying to us about being off heroin?*

Distracted by these thoughts, Sara saw the accident only from the corner of her eye. Her little sister whipped her hand out of her brother's grip, rushed with full force to greet Sara, and fell on the ice, face down, legs splayed. At once Sara saw her bruised cheeks, and her bottom lip beginning to bleed.

"I want Mommy!" Rachel screamed.

"Baby!" Robbie taunted.

Sara knew she could never take her mother's place. "Help me lift your sister," she said calmly to her brother. And to Rachel she said, "Mommy will be home in a little while."

Sara was glad her mother wouldn't be rushing out after supper to her second job, the one she'd taken after Sara's father died. "As long as I'm putting bread on the table and we have a roof over our heads," Helen told the children, "I won't work weekends. At least we'll have that time to spend together."

If I only knew why Daddy couldn't stop taking heroin without killing himself.... If I only knew why he got hooked on drugs in the first place.... Maybe my nightmares would end; maybe the images would fade away. Her recurring bad dream had taken on new hues: Her father promised to feed her, Robbie, and Rachel tutti frutti ice cream for breakfast. Then he turned into King Kong, kidnapped them, and left them hanging on meat hooks in his butcher shop freezer. *Just thinking about it gives me the creeps,* Sara thought. *Should I tell Ma what's bothering me? Or will that make things worse? Since the funeral, Ma's been so distant and busy, smoking too much, coughing in fits, lost in a world of her own.*

"We're home," Sara said to Robbie and Rachel as she unlocked the double door locks. And she thought to herself, *I have to talk to Ma tonight.*

The living room was in disarray, boxes stacked on the rug, old photographs strewn everywhere—on the couch, the coffee table, the credenza. Startled by the sight, Sara wondered if she'd entered the wrong apartment. *What's going on? This isn't the way Ma usually leaves the house. She keeps everything so neat and tidy. And where's Whiskers? The cat must be having a field day. Oh, there she is!*

"No, Rachel, get Whiskers out of that box. It's going to tip over. And you're too big for it." Sara wondered whether her mother intended to go through all these photos. "Let's move into the kitchen, kids."

"I'll find the cookies," Robbie offered. "I think we have Oreos."

When Helen's key opened the door at around five and she stepped into the apartment, Sara saw the weary, faraway look in her eyes.

"I fell and hurt my lip," Rachel said, jumping up and running toward her.

"Oh, *mamela,*" Helen said, patting Rachel on the head. She looked at Rachel's mouth and cooed, "It's OK now." She turned to Sara.

"What happened, dear?"

"A spill on the ice. She's all right. She cried for you."

"Rachel, dear, you know Sara can take care of you. Don't you, sweetie?"

Rachel looked up at her sister apologetically and then at Helen. "Yes, Mommy."

Helen added, "Let's thank Sara for getting you home safely, shall we, Rachel?" And in a voice just above a whisper, she said to Sara, "I wish you didn't have this job on top of your schoolwork. Where's Robbie?"

Sara hesitated. "He insisted on pushing through those boxes in the living room and watching TV. I had to collect the photos and set them aside."

"Oh, I meant to do that. Sorry." Helen walked like a windup toy into the kitchen to make supper. Sara followed.

"Can I help you with dinner?"

"You can open a can of salmon. Close the kitchen door so Whiskers doesn't come in."

"Why are the boxes out, Ma?"

"I want to remember the happy times," she said. She cracked an egg in a bowl, mixed it with matzo meal, and reached for the fish. "Did you see the photo of your father with his harmonica band?"

"I didn't have time to look through them, Ma. Maybe you'll show it to me. Can I talk to you after Robbie and Rachel go to bed?"

"About what?" She started heating oil in a skillet.

Sara hesitated.

"Please take out the frozen vegetables, will you, hon? Do you have much homework this weekend?"

"Well, that's just it, Ma. I have a make-up assignment."

"*You*?" Her mother came to attention. "A *make-up* assignment?"

"It's been bothering me. I can't get myself to do it. It's from when Daddy died and I missed school."

"You're such a good student—straight As. Just do it."

"That's what I want to talk to you about."

"What's to talk about? Do it."

"The assignment reminds me of Daddy. I get into a bad mood when I think of him."

"I've been getting blue, too," she said, popping the salmon cakes into the sizzling oil. "We both need to look at those photos and cheer up," she said. "We'll put together a Good Times album."

"Ma, I have questions for you...about Daddy's addiction."

"That's not going to improve your mood," she said.

"I want...no, I *need*, to know *how* Daddy got addicted and why he couldn't stop. Did it have to do with that man Spencer? And during the war, was he addicted then, too?"

"Sara, I don't want to hear any of that tonight. I've had too much *tsuris* from Grandma and Poppy. You know they blame me for everything. Thank God they're letting us stay in the apartment! I took those photos out to put us in a good mood. I have a plan for after we do the food shopping downtown on Sunday. I've arranged it all with Aunt Annette. We'll get over the hump, honey."

"But Ma..."

"Don't 'But Ma' me! Forget the vegetables. And forget about addiction. Do the make-up homework."

Is Ma crazy? How can I possibly forget Daddy's addiction?

Sara sat at the kitchen desk for almost an hour after dinner. Reading and rereading the textbook chapter on Roosevelt and World War II exhausted her. She pinched herself to stay awake. She reached for the new Nancy Drew mystery on the bookshelf but decided instead on the copy of William Blake's *Songs of Innocence and of Experience* that she'd had since fifth grade. She still liked reading Blake's poems aloud for school declamation contests. "A Poison Tree" was a favorite.

I was angry with my friend,
I told my wrath, my wrath did end.
I was angry with my foe;
I told it not, my wrath did grow.

"Who are you talking to?" her mother cried on the other side of the closed swinging door.

"No one," Sara shouted back. "I'm reading to myself."

"It's late," her mother said. "You can finish up tomorrow."

On Sunday morning, Helen rushed to drop off Sara's younger siblings around the corner with Aunt Annette and Uncle Nat. "Let's have some privacy, huh, cookie?" she said to Sara. We won't lug the kids along this time. I have some history to tell you. All about your father."

Sara couldn't have been happier. The day finally had arrived when her mother would reveal the secrets of her father's past.

Since Sara's father died, Helen had been taking the family to downtown Brooklyn on Sundays to do the food shopping. They'd pick up everything they needed for the week except for dairy, and then they'd take their time browsing in Mays and Abraham & Straus. Today, however, Sara and her mother moved quickly through the fruit and vegetable markets so they could wind up at Junior's Restaurant before the Christmas lunchtime crowd arrived.

Sara had never eaten at Junior's before and she didn't think her mom had either. Not only was it expensive, it hadn't been one of Josef's accounts, and it catered to a mainly Italian clientele. As Sara stepped through the restaurant's heavy doors, she felt as though she were sailing back in time. Helen surprised Sara by telling her that she first met Sara's father at this spot in 1937, when she was fourteen. "A popular soda fountain was located here," she said. "I had just passed the entrance exam to Walton High School, an all-girls' school in the Bronx. Your father was a year ahead of me at Eastern District."

Junior's didn't look like most of the restaurants in the area, from the mirrored walls and the bar stools clustered around a long, curving counter to the clock above the counter lit up by neon lights and the upholstered striped booths with matching red-and-white menus. For Christmas, a crèche had been set up beside the coatrack, where Helen hung up their jackets. After they found a booth and placed their shopping bags under the table, Helen walked over to the jukebox and sank eight quarters into the Wurlitzer. She waited to hear the first spin of "Heartaches" by the Ted Weems Orchestra, with Elmo Tanner whistling. Dewy-eyed, her mother returned to the booth saying, "We listened to this tune, your father and I, at the 1939 World's Fair. They called it 'The World of Tomorrow.' We saw Johnny Weissmuller dive into the huge pool at the Billy Rose Aquacade."

Some "tomorrow" Ma had with Daddy, Sara thought sadly.

"When your father and I used to meet here—it was just a malt shop then—we had such good times! I remember when I was sixteen, your father wanted to build me up as a beauty."

"Build you up as a beauty?" *What did that mean?* Sara was skeptical about these sugar-sprinkled stories cascading from her mother's lips. She wondered how long this nostalgic interlude at Junior's would last. Hearing the real truth about her father was uppermost in her mind.

"Your father thought I was hiding my looks in an all-girls' school," her mother said, taking a deep breath. "He wanted me to dress up—you know, to be on the fast track and in the groove like he was."

"Groove? Fast track?"

"He didn't want me to be a square. He said I'd waste away being a bookworm. But I knew I wouldn't waste away. I concentrated on schoolwork better around girls. I didn't want to attract silly boys or be sidetracked by riffraff. That's how we talked back then."

Their conversation was interrupted by their waiter. "What would you ladies like?" he asked, poised in black and white like a penguin, his pad ready.

"Go ahead, Ma. You first." Sara hoped the lunch might bring her mother back down to earth.

"I'll have scrambled eggs on a toasted English muffin and a cup of coffee," Helen said.

"Make it two," Sara said.

"You got it, ladies."

"Where was I?" her mother said. "Oh, yeah. I was shapely. I didn't want any wolf-whistle guys sniffing around me. So I dressed down and wore man-tailored suits."

"So Daddy was more than just a wolf-whistle guy?" Sara said, humoring her.

"He was the leader of the Detones," she said proudly, standing up her knife like an exclamation point. "That was the name of your father's harmonica band. They started playing *klezmer*, Jewish music, in the neighborhood. Sometimes they played for school dances. But a year after Benny Goodman's band headlined at Carnegie Hall, your father and his friends played jazz harmonica at all the local clubs. That was two years after we met, 1939. All the flashy girls at the soda fountain threw themselves at your father. They went crazy for him—his chiseled features, wavy hair. But he had eyes only for me."

Sara brooded. Would she ever be able to penetrate her mother's wall of memories and tease out the truth about the real life—the sad life—her mother had with her father? *Mom's leaving out the pain. She's not facing the way it really was. Can I do something to help her? But what?* She thought of the school guidance counselor. *Maybe Mrs. Rifkin can advise me.* But Sara rejected the idea, because Mrs. Rifkin didn't offer help to families. *Maybe Aunt Annette can suggest something.*

Their food arrived. Sara took a bite out of her egg sandwich. Her mother sprinkled salt and pepper on hers. "Believe it or not, your father was a good soul. Grandma called him a *gute neshumah* because he carried heavy shopping bags up flights of stairs for his neighbors. He helped his parents and his neighbors write letters in Yiddish to their families overseas. He was a good person."

Sara couldn't restrain her annoyance any longer. "If he was so smart," she said snidely, "then why didn't he go to college? His family could have afforded it. They owned a butcher shop."

"He *was* smart," her mother insisted. "Smart enough to help all the neighbors' children with their homework." With a shaky hand, she spilled her coffee. She soaked it up with a napkin, then looked at Sara. "But I told you, he didn't like being square. The squares went to college."

"That's ridiculous, Ma, to call young people squares if they wanted to get educated. You can't be proud that Daddy never went to college. Don't you want me, Robbie, and Rachel to go to college?"

"Of course I do, sweetheart, but times are different now. You just don't understand. Your father got involved with a different crowd."

"Mom, you're not facing the truth!" Sara's voice rose. She could not control her irritation, and oblivious to the people seated nearby, she said, "Why are you so determined to make Daddy out to be so perfect now that he's dead? Your whole married life with him, you thought his life had turned terrible, and you wanted to keep his shameful story hidden."

"Shhh!" her mother insisted, her finger on her lips. Like a nervous bird, she looked around the restaurant. "No one needs to know what goes on behind closed doors!"

"Mom, face it!" Sara insisted. "You're keeping *lies* behind closed doors, not personal confidences. Daddy lied that he was getting better. You're lying now about your past."

"I'm not lying, Sara. How I met Daddy, and the man he was—that's no lie."

"Why can't you tell me what I want to know?" Sara demanded. "I want to know how he got hooked on drugs, and I want to know why he couldn't stop! Why can't you tell me that?"

"That's all in the past now," her mother said, her voice trembling. "Keep your voice down, Sara. We have to move forward now."

"Move forward? It's only been a month! What's happened to your anger, Mom? I'm angry. Aren't you angry, too? Look what you had to go through. Where is your anger at Daddy for ruining our lives? Your anger at Grandma and Poppy for turning against us? How can you still be painting pretty pictures of the ugly life you had with Daddy? I saw it with my own eyes. How can you just swallow it and say it's the past?"

"Stop this, Sara! You're giving me a headache," her mother cried, coughing, holding her head in her hands. "Some things have to be buried so we can live."

"No! We can't bury lies! Not before we tell the truth. The lies aren't real. I'm worried. The only way that anger ends is to let it out. I learned that in school. You can't possibly be left with only happy memories. Think about it, Ma. Think about why you kept Daddy's life a secret. Why?"

"To protect you!" she shouted. She glanced around, realizing that all the tables and booths were filled. "I'm your mother," she said more softly. "I wanted to protect you from harm. And that's what I'm doing now. I'm protecting you from depression and grief."

"No, Ma. Fantasies don't protect anyone. We've got to accept what was. You kept his addiction secret because you were ashamed. You wouldn't have been so ashamed if he was so good and smart like you're making him out to be. If he was so good and smart, why did he bring so much trouble to our family? What's come over you, Ma? Why can't you acknowledge what he did to you? To all of us?"

Completely frustrated by her mother's resistance, Sara was about to suggest that they leave when a group of boys burst into the restaurant, shouting for drinks at the counter. "Heartaches" was still playing on the jukebox. The hooligans yanked the plug out of the jukebox, yelling, "What's this shit?"

"My music!" Sara's mother shouted. "What's going on?"

Sara recognized the leather jackets. As they blasted their transistor radios and started hopping from table to table, Sara remembered exactly who they were—the rocky crowd—the roughneck boys of the Eastern District, some from her history class, some who hung out near her apartment on Penn Street, and all marching toward the booth where she and her mother sat. "You the ones playing that shit on the jukebox?" one of the teenagers shouted, his long, dark hair slicked into a DA. Sara knew who he was—the ringleader.

Her mother shot back, "I've got another quarter in that machine. You owe me."

The boy laughed in her face.

"Waiter!" her mother shouted. "Waiter! Get this piece of *dreck* out of here."

The gang leader started to reach for her mother's pocketbook. Sara's shouts stopped him. "Johnny Rigo! I know who you are!"

Behind the counter, the restaurant owner yelled, "The police are coming! You bastards."

Johnny Rigo took a long look at Sara. "Mr. Carney!" he said nervously.

"Yeah," Sara said. "You were suspended, but I'll see to it that Carney has you expelled."

"Nah," Johnny Rigo snarled, knocking their plates off the table with a sweep of his arm. "You bitches ain't worth it," he shouted. He swiveled around and rushed his gang out of the restaurant.

The shrill sound of police sirens filled the restaurant.

"Sara," her mother said, "are those the boys you used to sneak out at night to see on Penn Street?"

Sara looked away. How could she ever have thought any one of them was cute?

"Promise me you won't hang out with them. They're no good. They're not for you. Believe me, I know. I know what happens to latchkey boys when they get into gangs. They have no motivation for school. They feed on ways to get into trouble." She reached for Sara's hand across the table.

"How do you know about gangs?" Sara asked.

Helen fussed with a napkin. An officer approached their booth. "You ladies OK?"

"We're all right," Helen said. "Just shaken up."

Sara told the officer she knew the ringleader, and the officer took down her information

When the officer left, Sara continued, "Was Daddy in a gang that used drugs?"

All the color left her mother's face. She took a cigarette from her pocket book, lit up, and began to cough.

Sara worried about her mother's health. *Ma must be carrying my father's story in every cell of her body,* she thought. Her mother's body was afflicted with a condition she called *nerves,* nerves which she had tried to settle, unsuccessfully, by becoming a chain smoker. Now that Josef was gone, her chronic cough had gotten worse, and she wheezed a lot. Sara believed her mother needed to fully unburden herself, so she repeated her question. "Ma, did Daddy's gang use drugs?"

"None of us, not me, not Grandma or Poppy, really knew then what was going on with him," she replied. "I realize now that your father can't be totally blamed for what happened to him."

"How can you say it wasn't Daddy's fault? He became an addict, destroyed his family, created so much suffering—and you say he's not to blame? He did belong to a gang, didn't he?"

"I can't talk about it."

"Oh, Ma, you promised! I have to know! Please."

Helen took a long drag on her cigarette. Finally she said, "It wasn't that the gang used drugs, but those boys *led* him to drugs. If it weren't for those roughnecks, who knows? Your father might not have become addicted and might still be alive." Her mother buried her head on the table and started crying.

Between sobs, she managed to go on. "Hoodlums—Irish and Italian gangs at Eastern District—splashed a swastika with red paint on Poppy's shop window. Your father pleaded with Grandma and Poppy to go to the authorities, but they didn't want to complain. After that, your father was never the same. All he could think was, *This is America, and my parents are still too afraid to call the police.*"

"Are you saying Daddy became an addict because of anti-Semitism? That doesn't make sense."

"Anti-Semitism drove him out of school because the gangs there were picking on Jews. He and his friends didn't want to fight with them—Daddy's group wasn't the fighting kind. They decided to play hooky and spent all their time setting up the Moonglow Clubroom. They didn't use drugs, either—but they smoked reefer. I never saw it, because they did it after the curfew, eleven o'clock, when all the good girls like me had to be home."

"So then where did Daddy get heroin in the first place?"

With tears streaming down her face, Helen said, "In Harlem. He fit right in, with his zoot suits and wing-tipped shoes. He got hooked in the Savoy Ballroom where he played swing on his harmonica with the bands. He tried to hide it from me. We broke up two or three times. Oh, what he did to himself." She took large gulps of water. "He took his music and his fancy outfits up to Harlem, and with Spencer, another high school dropout, he threw all our dreams down the drain."

"So that's where it happened," Sara said, shaking her head. "In Harlem." She paused. "I remember it was Spencer's wife who first told you Daddy was on drugs again."

"Let's go," Helen said, sweating. "We'll talk more when we get home." She paid the bill and left a tip.

The Kent Avenue bus was crowded with shoppers, but luckily Sara and her mother found seats. Helen held Sara's hand and talked openly about things she'd locked up for years. Sara learned how her father's truancy and his playing harmonica in nightclubs made him easy prey for pushers in Harlem. Still, the details of how exactly he got hooked and the reason he couldn't stop taking heroin remained a puzzle to her. They were so engrossed in their talk that they almost missed their stop.

Once in the apartment, though, Helen was too tired to continue. She dragged herself to the bedroom for a nap, saying all the excitement had made her dizzy.

Sara opened a bottle of soda and sat down at the kitchen desk where she had left her school bag. She was ready to complete Mr. Carney's make-up assignment. She took out her history textbook and once again began skimming the chapter on World War II: the large debts Germany owed after World War I, the rise of the Nazi Party, the Nazi occupation of Poland, and the bombing of Pearl Harbor. Important as she knew these events were, they meant little to her, so how could she write about them?

Chewing on a fingernail, Sara's mind kept returning to her mother's account. A story was forming in her mind, one that she wanted and needed to write. Could she submit *that* story—her father's story—as her history assignment? Why not? Her father's problems started in the Depression while Roosevelt was president, and her father served in the war. She stood up and paced in the kitchen. *So what if it's not exactly what Carney asked for? Couldn't my idea be better than a dry summary of the facts? Isn't a story based on real life a form of history?*

Sara sat down and began writing what came out of her head. When she was finally finished, she wrote at the top of the first page: "What Happened to My Father, Josef Katz, While Roosevelt Was President."

It wasn't *all* true, but it wasn't all fiction either.

Chapter Fifteen | 1964

"Sara, I beg you, don't do it!" Helen cried from the kitchen.

Sara heard her mother's cry, then the shuffle of her terrycloth slippers on the linoleum. "What's going on, Ma? You're not dressed yet?" In the bleak winter light, Sara could make out her mother hovering over something on the table, her floral housedress hanging loosely on her small figure.

"This report! I won't let you hand it in."

"You stole my homework assignment!" Sara shouted, watching her mother finger the precious pages. "That report isn't meant for you. You read it without my permission!"

"It was hanging out of your school bag," her mother said. "I saw the title..." She nervously fussed with her hair. "You wrote it without *my* permission. Sara, you're not handing this report in! I won't let you."

Sara walked over to the kitchen window, where a gray rain sounded on the pane, then back to the table, where she gathered the stray pages of her report. Sara felt her mother's eyes on her.

"Sweetheart," her mother softened, "it's a touching story. Don't get me wrong. You're only a high school junior and already such a good writer. I can't believe you actually put it together from what I told you. But there's too much personal information in it. Please tell me you won't bring it into school the way it is."

"I have to," Sara said firmly, slipping her arms into her peacoat and wrapping a woolen scarf around her neck. "It was due last Friday, and vacation starts tomorrow! If I don't submit it today, I'll get a zero. My record will be ruined."

"Your record with *me* will be ruined, Sara, if you dare to hand that in." Casting a glance into the foyer, her mother called out to the younger children. "Kids, your sister is ready to leave. Put on your boots and take your umbrellas." And to Sara she said vehemently, "If I knew you were going to share any of our private business with your teacher, I wouldn't have told you anything."

Facing the foyer mirror, Sara saw her own blue eyes narrow, her forehead fill with worry lines. *Could it be that Ma is right? Maybe Mr. Carney won't even accept this assignment. He's an old-fashioned history teacher who's been at Eastern District forty-two years. He may hate this.*

Pushing her qualms aside, Sara said, "You'll have to trust me, Ma. What I'm doing is not wrong. Why can't you just trust me?" Sara kissed her mother's cheek before leaving the apartment, her siblings in tow.

"Sara!" her mother said, before closing the door. "I don't want to be disappointed when I come home from work tonight."

Once she was sitting at her wooden desk in homeroom, Sara reread her overdue report. Before the first period bell sounded, she wrote a cover letter to Mr. Carney.

December 23, 1963
Dear Mr. Carney,
I'm submitting my make-up assignment for "How Did President Roosevelt Lead the United States into World War II?"—except I couldn't write it the way you wanted. I tried over and over to use the textbook to answer your question, but I kept blanking out. I mean, I wasn't able to concentrate. I kept being distracted by a real story that took place when Roosevelt was having trouble with the Depression and the war. It's the story of my father and how his life got ruined back then. I just had to write my father's story because he died early this month, and I can't get him out of my mind. His photos are everywhere in our apartment. At the desk in the kitchen, where I finished my report over the weekend, my father's troubled face stared at me from the last photo we took of him, peering out the window of his car. How he cherished that car, Mr. Carney, even at the end of his illness, his two-tone Cadillac, with white-walled tires.

My report is in story form. We've been writing stories in Miss Newman's English class. Sometimes she's even given me an A. I imagined myself a story writer for your assignment, giving my characters words to say. My mother's been filling me in on what happened to my father, but she hasn't been very well since the funeral, and she's been speaking to me in dribs and drabs. Then this weekend she poured her soul out to me. With her information—and our textbook—I came up with a story. It's based on real life, but whenever I didn't know something, I made it up so it would fit.

I must tell you that my mother is completely against my handing this in. I don't know what she's afraid of. She says it's shameful, but it's the only assignment I can turn in, and I can't believe that telling the truth can be bad. I've marked the confidential information in red so you'll know what has to remain private. I hope you'll accept it. I stayed up all night writing this in order to meet your deadline, and I've written much more than the five pages you assigned.

Even though it's in story form, you'll see that I do understand the conditions that Roosevelt was dealing with—the Nazi threat, the pressure on the United States to enter the war, and the growing hatred of Jews, even in our country.

My father lived through it all.

Sincerely,

Sara Katz

P.S. I know you told the class never to use a death in the family as an excuse, but this time it's *true*. I couldn't get words out of my mouth the day I came back to class after my father's funeral and stood at your desk, so you never really learned what happened to me.

What Happened to My Father, Josef Katz,
While Roosevelt Was President

Our textbook doesn't tell us how frightened the young men were of dying when Roosevelt called the country to war. Frightened and confused. Those boys had to put up a big front to act brave. It was even harder for Jewish boys, because fights were breaking out right here in Brooklyn, where Jews were hated. And with all the fears those young men had, some were bound to find ways to escape. I want you to know how my father tried to escape from the pressures he was feeling. The cold, narrow hole he burrowed into never allowed him to crawl out. At first my father was ready to fight against the Nazis, but his faith in our country got broken, and he didn't want to die for nothing. My mother began to notice my father's upset as early as 1939 when they heard Father Coughlin on the radio blaming the Jews for the war in Europe. My father read the nasty columns about Jews in the newspapers and overheard the snide comments on the streets. He was a junior at Eastern District at that time. What he loved the best was playing in a harmonica band. Mr. Carney, I wonder if you knew my father—Josef Katz.

My mother told me that family problems weighed heavily on my father's mind. His parents were deeply worried that their cousins in Poland were being starved and persecuted by the Nazis or were possibly dead. My father wrote letters in Yiddish that were sent overseas, but the family received no response. They made many calls to Europe that didn't get through. They appealed to the Hebrew Immigrant Aid Society on the Lower East Side, but their cousins couldn't be located.

Clouds of sorrow hung not only over my grandparents but over my father as well. He tried to help neighbors whose relatives overseas were threatened. He was good at learning languages, and he took French in school, so he did favors for his French neighbors by writing to their families in France. Some of his neighbors came from Germany, and he could write in German, too.

German is a lot like Yiddish. They would tell him what they wanted to say, and he'd put it down the way it was supposed to be written. My father started out a sensitive man, heartsick over the persecution of his fellow Jews in Europe. According to my mother, when my father heard that Cash and Carry was passed—Roosevelt's plan to help the Allies—my father figured that Churchill was convincing Roosevelt to enter the war. When Roosevelt set up the first draft for men twenty-one to thirty-five in 1940, my father—who was still in high school—told my mother that younger men would be next, and he'd have to decide very soon what he was going to do. My father was in great conflict. My grandparents understood it was my father's duty to fight, but they didn't want to lose their only son to war. You see, my father's older brother Alex had already died, crushed under a trolley, a brother my father never knew. So my grandparents overprotected my father, wanted to keep him close. He told my mother that he often felt smothered living under his dead brother's shadow.

My father's life became more troubled when anti-Jewish feeling began springing up right here in Williamsburg. Irish and Italian kids my father knew in school, former friends and acquaintances, began forming gangs and labeling my father and his harmonica buddies "dirty *yids*." My father's Jewish friends weren't used to getting into brawls. They wanted nothing to do with knives and chains. But my father had to do something when someone painted a bright red swastika on his father's butcher shop window.

You probably remember, Mr. Carney, that these kinds of things were happening while Roosevelt was president. I'm not saying he was responsible, but these incidents were part of his time. I can imagine how horrified my father and grandparents felt seeing that swastika on their window. They probably were just as horrified as the families of those black girls you told us about who were killed by the KKK in the Alabama church bombing not too long ago, or the black families in the South who found KKK crosses burning on their lawns. Racism can be terrifying, especially if you don't trust the authorities to do anything about it.

I can imagine the conversation between my grandparents and my father. "We lived through this before, son, in the *pogroms* in Russia," my grandmother would have said.

My grandfather spoke in Yiddish. "It's better to just let this blow over. I'll wash the paint off."

But my father was determined to bring the culprits to justice. "You can't let this happen and do nothing, Pop. This isn't Russia under the czar. We're in America now. We have rights here. And you should speak English."

"Rights?" my grandfather said. The idea of people having rights was foreign to my grandfather. I can see him rocking his head in his hands, repeating, "Rights? Rights?" I see him placing his hands on my father's shoulders, looking him squarely in the eyes, his own eyes filling with tears. His voice chokes as he says, again in Yiddish, "For us Jews, believe me, there are times—I know all about them—when what you call rights don't mean anything, anywhere—not even in America."

I can imagine him wiping his tears with his bloodstained butcher apron and slowly walking to the back of the store searching for a wash basin. "The paint has to come off," he says.

I picture my father following him, kicking up sawdust and pounding his fist on the butcher block. "No, Pop, you're wrong. Rights mean something here. You can't accept this treatment." My grandfather returns with the basin and wet rags for washing off the paint. At that moment my grandfather might have appeared smaller and frailer to my father than ever before. In my grandfather's sad frame, my father might have seen his own dreams of freedom, justice, and opportunity threatened.

So you see, Mr. Carney, discrimination against Jews was a reality in our own country, not only in Europe. It existed during Roosevelt's administration, and my father was deeply troubled by it. It made him disillusioned in America.

A very sad thing happened next. Because my father did not want to fight anti-Semitic ruffians at school, my mother tells me that he stopped going to school. And it's here, I must ask you, Mr. Carney, to keep the rest of this story confidential—everything I've marked in the margin with red pencil. My mother doesn't want to advertise the ugly truth about my father's truancy and delinquent behavior or her own disobedience. I can hardly believe it myself: my father a high school dropout and my mother lying to her parents. My father would have been shocked, even outraged, if I had decided to quit school. After my father saw that the gangs were challenging him and his friends for being "stuck-up" Jews, for having big heads and thinking they were better than everyone else, he decided he had had enough of classes and playing harmonica for school dances. He decided that playing hooky and playing music in clubs were much more rewarding.

My father never told my mother about the Moonglow Clubroom on Lee Avenue until its doors were opened. So she didn't know about his hooky playing until much later. Like the Crow's Nest, the Jester, and Club Cimarron—the other clubs in the city's ethnic neighborhoods—the Moonglow, I learned, was a rented basement apartment where high school boys spent evenings mingling and dancing, jamming on their instruments, drinking booze, and smoking cigarettes and reefer. Yes, Mr. Carney, they smoked marijuana back then. The Moonglow consumed all my father's time and energy. But after it was set up, most of my father's friends returned to school. Not my father.

My mother learned about the blow-up after it happened. Kevin Shea, the leader of an Irish gang, carried a gun, so when he and some of his buddies came into the Moonglow looking for trouble, my father, who carried a knife, got designated as the bouncer. My father told Shea it was a private club. He saw the bulge on Shea's leg and said, "We don't want fights here."

"We're just here to see what you got," Shea said and drew the pistol from under his slacks. My father was a head shorter than Shea and lighter in weight. He tried yanking the gun out of Shea's hand, but he couldn't flip it out of his grip. Shea struck my father's forehead with it and threw him off balance. Somehow, my father managed to rebound and tug the gun out of Shea's hand. It fell to the ground, and Shea reached for it. In that second, my father swept his jackknife over Shea's thigh, gashed it, and picked up the gun. Realizing he was wounded, Shea said, "Enough," and, luckily for my father, he hobbled off, leaning on his friends' shoulders. Shaken by the event, my father resolved to stay away from school where he might run into Shea and his gang. Because my father's classes were large, and his friend Davy Pollack punched in his Delaney cards for him, my father wasn't missed in school…initially. He was even able to pass his exams without going to class.

I can hear his good friend Davy plead with him. "Are you crazy, man? I care about you. You'll be expelled if you're caught out of school."

"Just don't tell Helen," my father says. "She doesn't know about the club yet. I haven't told her I dropped out."

"Your own girl, and you haven't told her? What's the matter with you?"

My father, for over a year, told neither his parents nor my mother about his truancy. My mother never suspected, since she attended a different school than my father, a high school for girls in the Bronx. All that time, my grandparents thought my father was a model student because he was smart and got good grades. They imagined him to be the perfect son who was making up for Alex, the six-year-old son they lost.

My mother told me that before she learned about my father's truancy, she liked going to the Moonglow Clubroom with him. She was rebellious herself, since her parents didn't allow her in a clubroom. They thought clubrooms were dimly lit basement hangouts where good girls lost their reputations.

My mother didn't want to give up the Moonglow—listening to my father play the harmonica with his band, the Detones; dancing the Shim Sham Shimmy and the Lindy Hop to swing and bebop recordings; rehearsing acrobatic routines for the citywide contests held in Harlem at the Savoy Ballroom. But she had strong doubts, too. How long could she continue lying to her parents? What if they found out she'd been going to the club? What if they learned that Josef smoked reefer? I was flattered, Mr. Carney, that my mother trusted me enough to tell me these things about her life as a teenager. So please don't share this information with anyone else.

Finally, when my father was a senior, he told my mother that he had dropped out of school and wasn't being allowed to graduate. She remembered their argument.

"The know-how I've picked up on the streets makes up for everything," he said.

"Don't be ridiculous," she said. "You'll ruin your life. You'll regret it."

"There's no guarantee life will be easy with a diploma," he shot back. "If I have to choose between graduating and learning about life, I'll pick life hands-down."

My mother was speechless.

"What do you think I do on Fifty-Second Street when I go to Kelly's Stables? Do you think I just listen to the piano player and watch Charlie Chaplin movies? Or when I go to Oscar's Bar? Do you think I just sit and drink vodka while

I munch on hard-boiled eggs and onions? I play harmonica. I make contacts. For God's sake, Helen, I have an audition with Borrah Minevitch and the Harmonica Rascals. They're making a movie!"

My mother realized then that the man who had been courting her, the one she pictured herself marrying and making babies with, had his head in the air—a *luftmentsch,* she called him. She asked herself why he was making life harder for himself. Why wasn't he staying in school until he graduated? Why didn't he master his parents' trade and open a butcher shop in the neighborhood the way he used to dream about?

My mother found out that my father's buddy, Spencer, the guy who lived nearby on Bedford Street and used to ask my father for help with his homework, played hooky with him. They traveled together to the Savoy Ballroom on Lenox Avenue, where the Savoy Sultans let my father jam with them during rehearsals because they knew he was good. Al Cooper, the band leader, told my father, "Boy, you got a great sound. Where the hell did you come from?" And that was it. It wasn't about color. It was about respecting people's talents.

My father told my mother he found relief at the Savoy Ballroom, relief from the racial tension in the city and his own personal problems. He liked mixing socially with people of different backgrounds and being transported by the music out of his worries and fears.

I can see my father at the Savoy Ballroom watching some of the Sultans get high on weed, smack, and pills. When he was at the Moonglow, he went no further than drinking vodka and smoking reefer. But at the Savoy, I imagine him in the men's room with a pusher telling him that booze is a downer and he should try a different groove. He knows that Spencer tried smack a few times, but my father is scared of it. The risks of heroin begin filling my father's head. He'll shame his family, lose my mother, and maybe become addicted. He knows boys in the neighborhood who've gotten hooked and become ill.

The pusher says to my father, "C'mon, man. Fuck. Hang up that jive. Just horn this, snort it."

My father tells him to get lost. "I don't want any shit," he says.

"You're drinking like there's no tomorrow," the pusher says. "But when you sniff this stuff, you got no hangover and your instrument sings like a bird."

"Guys die from smack," my father says, pushing the guy away.

A few other players on break walk into the men's room. They catch on. I hear a lanky trumpet player say to my father, "None of us is hooked, my man. Right, guys?"

"Yeah," the other players say.

The trumpet player continues. "With smack, you can taste and just play around. Some guys don't know when to stop. But that doesn't have to be you. You just stop when you want to, like we do. Why don't you just try it?"

My father is about to leave and get a drink with Spencer, when the trumpet player whispers in his ear. "You play your harmonica real good, sonny. Joey, we'll show you the way to go. Then you can play with us in the second set. What do you say, boys? Can't pretty Joey be big time with us?"

The players begin chanting, "Joe-eee! Joe-eee! Joe-eee!"

My father feels like getting high. *What's wrong with just tasting? I won't get hooked from a taste. Spencer's not hooked. If there's a problem, I'll stop. What the hell—I drink booze and smoke reefer. There's no harm in them.*

Mr. Carney, this is how I imagine my father is about to be hooked on heroin. I had to stop writing when I came to this part of the story because I was too overwhelmed. I had trouble seeing what I was writing through my tears. I was so upset, but I had to do your assignment! I wish I could have been there in the bathroom with my father. I wish I could have stopped him from snorting heroin that first time. I would have said to him, "Dad, don't ruin your life and everything beautiful that's ahead of you. What about the family you want to have someday, your children? Don't risk it, Dad! No, Dad. Turn your back!"

The trumpet player takes him into a stall and shows him how to snort powdered heroin. My father's sinuses begin to tingle and burn. His throat tastes bitter. He thinks he's made a big mistake. But when he steps onto the bandstand, and the drug begins to course through his body, he experiences an incredible high. He feels blissful, at peace. His demons are put to rest: the watchful, judging eyes of his parents; the haunting memories of his dead brother and his lost Polish cousins; the scorn of Jew-hating gangs; the war looming before him. High on heroin and the rhythms of swing, he soars for miles. The velvety chords streaming out of his harmonica sound perfect. He sees my mother in his mind, his Helen, floating above him on angel's wings. And his joy, his happiness, lasts all night. No fear or danger touches him. He's eighteen and free, invincible.

Free to be himself, the person he desires to be. And he wants to feel this way again and again.

That's what I imagine, Mr. Carney. One taste was too much for him. A taste that he needed to repeat for over twenty years because he couldn't stop. And he died from it.

Chapter Sixteen

Sara handed out candid shots of President Kennedy to the three other honors students in Mr. Carney's American history class. The photos captured the president at the March on Washington in August 1963. Sara participated in that march with other officers of the student General Organization at Eastern District High School. Only three months later, the president was assassinated, and Sara's own father died. In Sara's mind the two deaths fused. *First the president falls, then my father falls, and then, as in Ring Around the Rosy, we all fall down, the whole group of us wishing there could be better tomorrows—civil rights workers, people lobbying for jobs and freedom, peaceniks protesting war and nuclear proliferation, and mixed-up kids from troubled families like me...and that character I'm reading about, Holden Caulfield.*

She glanced at the bulletin board at the rear of the room, where Mr. Carney had hung portraits of all the presidents, from Washington to Kennedy. Seeing the empty space where Lyndon B. Johnson's portrait eventually would be placed, she began worrying. *What will happen to our country without President Kennedy...and what will happen to my family without my father? They were both so young—the president forty-six, my father forty-two. Was there only one person responsible for our president's assassination...and will I ever know the whole story of my father's death?*

Sara couldn't stay focused for long on Kennedy, though, because she kept thinking about the overdue assignment she had submitted to Mr. Carney. Even though Mr. Carney had asked Sara to write about the wartime policies of President Franklin Delano Roosevelt, Sara hoped Mr. Carney would grant her some leeway.

Mr. Carney smiled faintly at Sara from behind his desk. "See me after class, Miss Katz."

Sara opened her notebook. She glanced at the clock above the bulletin board at the back of the room. The minute hand was moving slowly. *How can I possibly wait until class ends? I'm so eager to know what Mr. Carney thought about my assignment!*

"Let's discuss President Kennedy's accomplishments," Mr. Carney continued.

Sara raised her hand. "He was the first Catholic president. And he tried to end racial segregation."

"Good, Miss Katz. Anyone else?"

Not seeing another hand raised, Sara spoke again. "He created the Peace Corps, too." And before Mr. Carney responded, she added, "I'd like to volunteer for service in Africa one day."

Anthony Spinelli shouted from the back of the room, a comb in his ear, his hand in a fist, "Go, Sara! We'll miss your fat ass!"

Several students laughed. "Back to order," Mr. Carney growled, whacking a yardstick on his desk. "Enough, Mr. Spinelli, or you'll wind up like Johnny Rigo—expelled."

He's getting back at me, Sara thought, looking in Anthony's direction where the rough boys sat, *because I complained to the principal about Johnny.*

"What about the Cold War and the Cuban missile crisis?" Mr. Carney asked. "How did Kennedy handle those?"

No matter where the discussion twisted, Sara kept returning to Kennedy's social justice policies and to his call to young people: "Ask not what the country can do for you..." Mr. Carney, who loved ancient history, told the class Kennedy took the words from Pericles. When the bell finally sounded, Sara stepped up to Mr. Carney's desk. "You wanted to see me, Mr. Carney?"

He handed her report to her. It felt like hot coals in her hands. "Miss Katz, you've certainly given me an account of the late 1930s and the drug culture your father unfortunately got mixed up with." His voice was low, serious, baritone. "But *gurl, 'tis* not what I asked *fer*. It doesn't fulfill the assignment on President Roosevelt." He coughed. "By the way, my sincere condolences on the loss of your father."

"Do you remember him, Mr. Carney?"

"Well, he was a student here twenty-five years ago. I regret my memory isn't what it used to be." He cleared his throat. "Miss Katz, I think your father's death is preventing you from focusing on American history. I understand how that can happen. I suggest that you—and your mother—see Mrs. Rifkin, the school guidance counselor. I set up an appointment for you on Friday morning. I think she can help both of you." He handed Sara a referral slip.

Sara's legs went limp. Her mouth opened and closed, but no words came forth.

"Are you OK, Miss Katz?"

Sara wanted to ask him if her homework was really so far off track that she needed guidance, but she couldn't muster the courage. Her ears began to sting. *I disobeyed my mother, got in trouble with my teacher, and now I'm being punished. Well, what did I expect? Carney's a stickler for rules.*

"I'm all right," she answered.

"You don't have to do the assignment again," Mr. Carney added. "Just make sure you study the chapters on Roosevelt carefully before the final."

"Yes, Mr. Carney." Her anger rose against him as she walked toward the lunchroom. *Why should I listen to him? He's no policeman. And I don't need a counselor. I'm not failing, and I'm not a discipline problem like Spinelli. What does Carney know? He's an out-of-touch old fart from the old school!*

The cafeteria smelled of overcooked vegetables and steamed rice. From her place in line, she peered into the crowded room. *Where is Larry?* She was supposed to meet him for lunch. As she filled her tray, her thoughts wandered. *How am I going to deal with Mr. Carney? Heck, if I had one of the new, young teachers, I'd be praised for doing an original assignment. Carney's such a jerk. He must have shown my paper to Mrs. Rifkin, even though I asked him not to share it with anyone. Ma's going to kill me. She'll say she told me so, and we'll fight again.* She looked around for Larry. *Maybe I won't say anything to Ma and just show up at Mrs. Rifkin's on my own.*

Sara liked Larry, the popular G.O. president, who was a year ahead of her. She had gotten to know him at the March on Washington. They sat together on the bus and took some photos of President Kennedy on the White House steps. Balancing her tray and book bag, Sara found Larry near the large basement windows and took a seat beside him. He was eating watery chow mein with a spoon.

"Sorry I'm late," she said.

"What's up?" he asked, as he spread a series of brochures on the table. "Here they are: State University of New York at Binghamton, William and Mary, Penn State. I'm considering all of them."

"I can't think about colleges now," she said. "Mr. Carney is sending me to the school guidance counselor."

"Really? Why? Isn't that for kids who are depressed or flunking out?"

"Mr. Carney's too damned strict," she said, noticing the concerned look on Larry's face. "Carney didn't understand a paper I submitted. It probably went over his head." She rolled her eyes in exasperation. "And now he wants Mrs. Rifkin to straighten me out."

Larry pushed his food tray aside. "Maybe when you see Rifkin, she can transfer you out of Carney's class next semester. Did you hear that Carney sent Joe Vogel to Mrs. Rifkin last year? He objected to Joe's being a G.O. officer—said it interfered with his studies."

"No kidding," Sara said.

"I don't think Carney likes student government. At least Mrs. Rifkin knows that the G.O. is important. She allowed Joe to transfer to another class."

Larry's words lifted Sara's spirits. In Larry, she saw the kind of young man she imagined her father must have been when he attended Eastern District during the Great Depression, before he stopped going to school and got hooked on heroin. Maybe her mother was right about the assignment after all; the picture she presented of her father was too negative.

Sara picked up Robbie and Rachel at school at three o'clock as usual, still obsessing about the appointment with Mrs. Rifkin. She sulked when she got home and performed her chores absent-mindedly. She took flounder out of the freezer for dinner, and with loud pings, the ice cube trays bounced onto the linoleum, splattering little squares of ice everywhere. Hearing the sounds, Robbie zoomed into the kitchen. Before Sara could stop him, he slipped on bits of broken ice and fell, ripping his corduroy trousers at the seams. Rachel insisted on helping Sara dry the floor. Bare-kneed, she crawled on the linoleum collecting ice cubes and, with a dish towel, soaked up wet patches. She wound up with a soiled dress and bruised knees.

When Helen got home, Rachel and Robbie were in the living room in their pajamas playing with a ball and jacks, puzzle pieces strewn on the rug and coloring books and crayons everywhere.

"What's happened here?" her mother asked Sara, seeing Robbie and Rachel ready for bed. "Are they sick?"

"No," Sara answered, sighing. "It was…a messy afternoon."

"Messy afternoon?" her mother repeated. The air between them felt thick to Sara. *Ma's gonna blow up when she hears about Mrs. Rifkin!* "I couldn't concentrate this afternoon, Ma. The kitchen floor, it got wet. Robbie slipped. Rachel hurt her knees."

"Why can't you concentrate, dear?" She touched Sara's hair affectionately.

"I have news about the assignment I handed in."

"You handed it in?" Her lips twitched. "What's your news?"

"It's complicated," Sara said turning toward the kitchen. "After dinner, OK? I'll dry the dishes while you wash."

"Oh no, young lady!" Helen said, taking hold of Sara's arm. "You tell me now." She steered Sara into the kitchen and sat her down at the table.

Breathing deeply, Sara told her mother about the appointment Mr. Carney set up with Mrs. Rifkin. Helen's cheeks flushed. Her head dropped. "Didn't I tell you something bad would come of this? It's just what I was afraid of."

Helen went to the pantry and pulled a pack of Chesterfields out of a carton. She walked to the kitchen window and lit a cigarette. The street lamps were just beginning to create hazy cones of light in the wintry darkness on Penn Street. "Now our personal business will spread around the school, and everyone will pity you! Or they'll have contempt for you. Our neighbors will know all our affairs."

"All you care about is your neighbors. What about me? I'm your child. Even dumb Mr. Carney knows I'm not OK."

"I *do* care about you, more than you realize. But one way or another, gossip gets out and you'll be hurt."

"How will I be hurt?"

"You'll be shunned." She took a long drag on her cigarette.

Sara's eyes widened. Oh, how she wished that she hadn't ruined everything.

Helen's voice rose. "Did *anyone* come forward at the funeral when Rabbi Korn asked the congregation for eulogies to your father?"

Sara looked her mother in the eyes. She *had* wondered why no one offered to speak at the funeral. Her father was known to many people, after all, being the son of the local kosher butcher.

"And the reason is," her mother continued, "the old-timers in our building were being polite. They knew your father wasn't living with us. And before that, when he was still with us, they'd see him stumble home at night, stoned. They watched from behind their curtains. On the street, I saw how they stared at him. They'd click their tongues, then lower their eyes. Yes, they were trying to be kind. What a change from how your father told me they used to praise him before his *bar mitzvah*. When he was a boy, they'd pinch his cheeks and call him a *gute neshumah,* a good soul."

Idealistic memories again, Sara thought.

Helen took a tissue from her pocket and began to dab her eyes. "Neighbors didn't speak at the funeral because they knew how low your father had sunk. But to us they were quiet. They gave us the silent treatment. And now that you couldn't control yourself, you're going to experience things that won't make you feel so good. To themselves, neighbors will call you *nebech,* and the kids at school will torment you. The Orthodox will avoid you altogether."

Sara listened to her mother's words, considering them. She remembered the odd look in Larry's eyes when she told him she was being sent to Mrs. Rifkin. Was it a look of pity? She shrugged off the idea. Sara was still convinced that if she and her mother wanted to move past her father's problem, they had to be open about it. "Ma, listen to me: No one in the neighborhood will have anything more to gossip about just because we talk with the guidance counselor."

"We're not talking to her," Helen said.

"What do you mean? Why not?"

"I don't believe in therapy. Not for someone my age."

"But, Ma! Who says it's therapy? Mrs. Rifkin is a school counselor, not a doctor. Look, if Mrs. Rifkin can't help you, maybe she can help me." Sara lost control. "Can't you see beyond yourself!"

"Don't open up a fresh mouth to me, young lady."

"But, Ma, I was hoping Mrs. Rifkin could help me concentrate on my schoolwork better. Maybe she could transfer me out of Mr. Carney's class."

After a few moments, her mother said, "Okay, maybe it would be good for you to have someone to talk to, Sara. You're too focused on your father's problems. But leave me out of it." She put out her cigarette.

"Look at you," Sara said. "You smoke like a fiend. Your cough never ends. You can't tell me Daddy's dying hasn't been a problem for you, too. I'm not the only one! You *have* to come with me. Mr. Carney made the appointment for both of us!"

"I can't possibly go on Friday. I work all day. Did you forget? I'll write a note for you to give to Mrs. Rifkin. You'll see what she has to say. Did you defrost the fish like I asked?"

An hour before homeroom on Friday morning, Sara walked down the long corridor on the third floor of Eastern District High School to deliver her mother's note to Mrs. Rifkin. She had no idea whether Mrs. Rifkin could really help her, or if Mrs. Rifkin would even meet with her without her mother being present. Though Helen scoffed at therapy, Sara knew intuitively that past problems needed to be dealt with, not buried, if they were to be resolved.

Could it be, Sara wondered, that her mother rejected anything resembling therapy because the Manhattan psychiatrist who treated her father with morphine turned out to be a fraud? Or did her mother fear that by seeing a counselor she'd be labeled as having a mental problem herself? Whatever the reasons, Sara felt angry at her refusal to see Mrs. Rifkin. In a way, she felt abandoned. She was reminded of the time her parents took off to Florida and left her with her aunt and uncle. Now her mother seemed to be leaving her again, this time to handle adult problems on her own.

On Mrs. Rifkin's door, there was a poster of Dr. Martin Luther King at the March on Washington. Sara felt relieved seeing the poster. She remembered her elation being part of the March on Washington with Larry Roth and the other G.O. officers. Dr. King's words, "I have a dream," inspired her to dream, too. Her father was still alive then and had approved of her taking the trip. As usual, her mother had said, "Your father doesn't always use good judgment." But Sara felt his judgment was quite sound then.

When Sara had seen Washington, D.C., for the first time from the bus window, with the magnificent trees and gardens, the classical buildings, and the reflecting pool on the National

Mall, she had been filled with surprise and wonder. And when she returned from the March, she shared her dream with her friend Ruth of going to an out-of-town college with vast green lawns, blossoming trees, and people filled with purpose. "That's a dream I don't dare to have," Ruth had said.

"What about a scholarship? Let's look into it. I'll help you find one." Ruth's dark eyes lit up like jewels.

Sara hoped Mrs. Rifkin would sympathize with her college ambitions.

"You must be Sara," Mrs. Rifkin said, opening the door. Sara saw a smiling woman of medium height with curly blonde hair. Mrs. Rifkin appeared to be around Sara's mother's age, in her early forties.

"Yes," Sara said, handing her a referral slip. "Mr. Carney sent me."

"I know. Please come in, sit down." She motioned Sara to the couch that faced her desk. An overfull magazine rack and a standing reading lamp stood beside the sofa. One wall was lined with bookshelves. A box of tissues sat on the coffee table.

"Will your mother be joining us this morning?"

"I almost forgot," Sara said, handing her mother's note to Mrs. Rifkin.

> January 2, 1964
> Dear Mrs. Rifkin,
> I cannot meet on Friday, as I am working. I tried convincing my daughter not to hand her report in, but she doesn't listen to me. I can meet with you on the weekend if necessary. I remain,
> *Mrs. Helen Katz*

"Very well," Mrs. Rifkin said looking up from the note. "You and I can chat now, Sara, just the two of us. Then, if the timing is right, you and your mother can see me again on Saturday morning. The school will be open for the PTA bazaar. How's ten-thirty? Will that work?"

"I'll have to ask my mother."

"Of course. If your mother can't make it, you and I can meet again before the end of the semester. I'll give you my telephone number." She handed Sara a slip of paper that had her name on it and the letters MSW. Sara would look up the abbreviation later.

"Do you know why Mr. Carney wants us to talk?" Mrs. Rifkin's voice was gentle, like a soft breeze.

Sara fidgeted on the couch. "Not really. I owed him a homework assignment that was late because my father died. My mother didn't want me to hand it in because she thought I included too much personal information that she was ashamed of. I told Mr. Carney to keep the homework confidential. Did he show it to you?"

"No, Sara. He said if I needed to see the report that I should ask you and your mother."

Sara's body relaxed. "That's good."

"What I'd like to know is why you handed the report in when your mother objected to it?"

"I had to do it for me!" Sara was surprised by the loudness of her own voice. She became self-conscious, not sure of what she should or should not say. "Excuse me, Mrs. Rifkin," she said.

"You did it for yourself. I see." Mrs. Rifkin looked at

Sara kindly. "Can you tell me what you mean?" She waited patiently.

Finally, Sara said, "My mother's never wanted me to talk to anyone outside our family about my father's problem. I don't even know if I should be talking to you about it now."

"Whatever you say is completely confidential."

Sara hesitated. "Well, OK. My father's sickness...hurt my whole family terribly, and when he died, instead of talking to me honestly about it, my mother went into a fantasy world of happy memories. That's not who she is. She frightened me. My performance in school started going downhill. I felt I had to be honest about what I knew. The writing just burst out of me!"

"You say your schoolwork wasn't going well," Mrs. Rifkin said thoughtfully. "Did you have a particular problem in Mr. Carney's class?"

Sara took some moments to think. "I wasn't able to concentrate in his class. I tried explaining to Mr. Carney several times why I was having difficulty, but I just couldn't get the words out. He's hard for me to talk to."

Mrs. Rifkin jotted some notes down in Sara's folder.

"When my father died, and I was out of class for a week, my make-up assignment was due. I couldn't hand it in on time because all I could think of was my father. So I had the idea finally to write *about* him. My father's life sort of overlapped with Mr. Carney's assignment. At least I saw it that way. But Mr. Carney is too narrow-minded to see the connection, I guess. He's too old-fashioned. My mother is, too—even though she's as young as you are."

Mrs. Rifkin laughed. "I'm glad you see me as young."

"Well, you think young if you support Dr. Martin Luther King."

"I see what you mean."

"My mother was angry that I wrote about my father to my history teacher. She's been upset with me ever since. Now she's doubly angry because you're involved."

"Maybe when your mother meets me, she'll see that I can offer some help."

The homeroom bell rang.

"OK, Sara. We have to finish now. This will have to be a short visit. Please ask your mother to let me know if the two of you can make it on Saturday."

"What if she asks me what happened today?"

"You can tell her that we met. Please assure her that I have not read your paper. You can tell her I asked you why you handed the paper in, but you don't have to say anything more. What we talk about together is just between us."

"What if she wants to know?"

"My goal is to have you and your mother communicate better with one another. If she had come with you today, I would have asked you the same question and asked your mother to listen without responding."

"You don't know my mother!"

Mrs. Rifkin laughed. "I hope to meet her soon."

When Sara told her mother that evening that the school guidance counselor still wanted to meet with her, Helen frowned. "Haven't I told you I don't want to see the counselor, Sara?"

It was after dinner and Sara was helping her wipe the dishes. Robbie and Rachel were playing Monopoly quietly in the living room. "No matter what the counselor says, Sara, I can't believe she hasn't read your report. She's going to question me about your father, and I don't want to talk about him."

"Mrs. Rifkin didn't read my report. She said she didn't need to read it because she wasn't interested in what was in it, only that I went against your wishes. All she wants is for us to communicate better."

"We don't need a guidance counselor for that. We need for you to have a little respect for my opinion, that's all." She blew her nose.

"She wants us to be together in her office. And so do I, Ma. I don't want to be in a fight with you. We can't seem to agree on anything lately. I want to understand you better, and I want to understand myself. I think Mrs. Rifkin can help. You don't have to talk about anything you don't want to."

"If I go with you—and it's just an 'if'—you're not going to dredge up the pain your father put us through."

"The session is just between you and me, Ma. About why we're not getting along. And how that's been affecting my schoolwork."

"Well, if the topic is us and how we're not getting along, how are you going to keep your father out of it?"

Sara threw up her hands. The phone rang. Her mother answered it.

"Yes, this is Sara's mother, Mrs. Rifkin..."

Chapter Seventeen

"I don't usually work at Eastern District on Saturdays," Mrs. Rifkin said. "But the school is open today...despite the storm they're predicting." She ushered Sara and her mother into her cozy, small office. "Come, ladies, sit down."

The guidance counselor was wearing a shaggy sweater and loose-fitting slacks, and her informal appearance pleased Sara. By contrast Helen wore a man-tailored suit, as if she were going to her sales job in downtown Brooklyn.

Mrs. Rifkin took her seat behind the desk. Sara and Helen sat on opposite ends of the naugahyde sofa across from her.

"This is the first time a school guidance counselor has asked to see me. Should I be concerned about Sara?" Helen asked, taking a cigarette from her purse with an unsteady hand.

"I didn't mean to alarm you on the phone last night, Mrs. Katz," Mrs. Rifkin said, taking an ashtray out of her desk drawer and offering it to Helen. "Your daughter has an excellent record and wants to achieve good things, but..."

"I realize Sara's upset," Helen interrupted. "But if you're going to recommend therapy, I don't trust it. Some years ago, my husband saw a psychiatrist. He wasn't any help at all."

Sara reacted quickly. "I tried telling my mother *this* isn't going to be therapy, Mrs. Rifkin. Anyway, the psychiatrist my father saw was a quack."

"Enough, Sara," Helen said, waving her hand dismissively. "See what she does?"

"I want to make something clear, Mrs. Katz. I'm not a therapist, and I assure you I'm not a psychiatrist. I'm a social worker who advises students. This isn't a therapy session, but it is a chance to help Sara." She paused, and in a sympathetic tone said, "Since your loss, Mrs. Katz, Sara's been disoriented without her father."

"Sometimes I wonder, Mrs. Rifkin, if Sara's father threw her more off course while he was alive." Helen's hand shook as she lit her cigarette.

"What do you mean, Mrs. Katz?"

"Sara's father was a successful kosher butcher. Wholesale and retail. Accounts all over the city. But sometimes..." she paused. "Sometimes he used bad judgment."

"Bad judgment?"

Helen took a drag on her cigarette. Smoke spiraled up in curls. "I saw the Martin Luther King poster on your door, Mrs. Rifkin. I didn't want Sara to go on that march. She went anyway, because my husband told her she could, even after I had forbidden her."

Mrs. Rifkin stepped to the window and opened it slightly, letting in the cold air. Snowflakes were beginning to fall. "I gather you and your husband didn't always see eye to eye."

Helen thought a moment. "He was more liberal than me. It's not that I'm prejudiced against colored people. Don't get me wrong. I just don't want to see my children getting hurt. Let other people stick their necks out." Her eyes searched Mrs. Rifkin's face.

"I see," Mrs. Rifkin said. "You don't approve of Sara's political activism."

"It's not just that. Sara and I lock horns over everything these days. She wants to talk about my husband's death all the time."

Sara's lips tightened.

"How long ago did he die?"

"A month ago."

"Well, a month is very recent, Mrs. Katz. Your emotions are still raw. If you and Sara can find a way to talk calmly to one another about the stress that inevitably comes up at a time like this, I think Sara will be able to get back on track. I'd like to help you achieve this."

Sara liked the way Mrs. Rifkin put things. She really wanted to get back on track. She realized Mr. Carney didn't like the make-up history assignment she handed in, but on the good side, her English teacher, Miss Newman, encouraged her to apply for a scholarship to universities with good writing programs. Yes, she wanted to get back on track because she wanted her mother to know she was thinking seriously about going to an out-of-town college when she graduated in a year. This was a subject she couldn't bring up easily while there was so much tension between them.

Mrs. Rifkin shuffled some papers on her desk. "Yesterday Sara told me why she submitted the make-up assignment. Perhaps you can talk about your objections."

"Have you read it?" Helen asked nervously.

"No, I haven't."

"I objected because...well, because the report contained inappropriate details about my husband's personal life and my own. Sara's history teacher—Mr. Carney—he must have sensed how inappropriate the report was. That's probably why he sent Sara to you."

"Why do you think your daughter disobeyed you, Mrs. Katz?"

"I know why. I don't have to think about it. She thinks she knows better than me about everything."

"No, I don't, Ma!" Sara said, making a face. "You always say that."

"Sara, this is your mother's time to talk," Mrs. Rifkin said gently. "It will help you to listen."

"Sara thinks that because we kept my husband's problem private while he was alive, now that he's dead we need to talk about it, even in casual conversation." Helen looked at Sara. "I'm trying to show her another way to deal with our loss."

"Can you explain?"

"Well, first we remember and honor the good times. Then we put the past behind us and get on with our lives."

"But you sugarcoat the past," Sara blurted out. "All those photos you unpacked and left around the living room! Daddy and you posing at parties with happy faces."

"What's wrong with that if it makes me feel better?"

"But it's a lie. There were more bad times than good!"

"Sara," Mrs. Rifkin interrupted, "please. It's your turn to listen. I guess, Mrs. Katz, you don't want to talk to Sara about the problems you had with her father?"

"Sara's been aware of her father's problem since she was eight years old," Helen began. Her body began to tremble. "She saw his decline. I wish I could have shielded her." She inhaled on her cigarette, pulled the ashtray toward her, and flicked the ashes. “Sara keeps asking me about her father’s past, about the time before she was born. At first, I didn’t think it was necessary for her to know. Shouldn’t children be proud of their parents? But she kept asking and asking. So, I shared some of her father’s shameful story, and right away she wrote about it. Without my permission.”

“Sara is sixteen now, a young adult, with adult questions. Doesn’t she have a right to know?”

“This is exactly why I didn’t want to come here,” Helen said, stubbing out her cigarette. “I didn’t want to delve into my husband’s problems.” She looked directly at Mrs. Rifkin. “So, what am I doing here?”

“You’re here to find a way to communicate with your daughter.”

Tears began rolling down Helen’s cheeks. Sara lifted a tissue from the box on the coffee table and handed it to her mother.

“You know, Mrs. Katz, you have every reason to be proud of your daughter. She’s bright, and she’s engaged in her school work. She’s college material. If she could just hear your point of view, I’m sure she’ll be able to understand why you don’t want to revisit the pain.”

After a number of rapid knocks on the door, a woman in her thirties charged into the office. A tag on her starched, white blouse read “Rose Cicarelli, PTA President.” She was out of breath. “Mrs. Rifkin, can you please come quickly to the gym? We’ve caught two boys stealing.” She looked around the office. “Oh, I’m sorry to interrupt.... We need you to identify them.”

Mrs. Rifkin rose from her desk. "Are the police there, Mrs. Cicarelli?"

"Yes, but they don't know who these young thugs are, whether they're students or outsiders."

Mrs. Rifkin turned to Sara and her mother. "Will you excuse me for a few minutes? Why not continue on your own? That's really why you're here. You can fill me in when I come back." Sara and Helen looked at one another apprehensively.

After a few moments, Helen said, measuring her words, a forced smile on her face, "Your Mrs. Rifkin is so very patient, so very easygoing. She thinks we can just smooth out our little wrinkles, just like that."

"Oh, Ma," Sara cried. "Mrs. Rifkin knows it's difficult. But we can make things better."

"What does she know? It's not *her* daughter airing dirty laundry out in public for everyone to see." She lit another cigarette.

"Ma, don't smoke again. It's bad for you."

"Don't tell me what to do!" Helen walked to the window for some air, perspiring and breathing heavily.

"Are you OK, Ma? Why don't you sit down?"

"You manipulated me. I don't want to be here. I've told you too much already." Helen moved to the door. "And don't you dare write another word about anything I've told you!" She put her suit jacket back on and lifted her coat off a hook on the wall. "I have shopping to do downtown."

"Ma, you can't leave. You're just getting started."

"I never wanted to come in the first place. I've had enough. Mrs. Rifkin will understand. It's just too painful for me."

Sara was pained and baffled by her mother's behavior. She had hoped this meeting would make their communication better, but now it seemed worse than ever. Once again, Sara had ripped her mother's wounds open. She had gone back on her word. She felt a heavy weight, a sense of betrayer's guilt. She was about to leave the office, not sure where she should go next, when Helen walked back in the door. "Ma, you're back!"

Snow dusted her hair and her face was troubled. "The police arrested the boys and took them away in the police car!" She was wheezing and placed her hand over her heart.

"Ma, sit down. Take off your coat."

"I'll keep it on. I can't take the cold lately. The snowstorm is getting worse."

Sara sat close to her mother on the couch. "What were you saying about the boys?"

"I saw that they were crying when the police caught them. They looked frightened and confused. I know they have to be punished, but I thought, *Did they really know what they were getting into when they pushed that lady and stole her pocketbook? Were they just trying to get attention?* And I remembered how your father looked when he needed a heroin fix. He also seemed like a lost boy. His blue eyes would dart all crazy, and he'd cry out for me to help him." She broke down in sobs.

"Oh, Ma," Sara said, embracing her. "You've been through so much."

"I was wrong for leaving so abruptly, Sara. Forgive me. All I want is that you not blame your father harshly. I realize now you'll continue blaming him if I don't tell you what really happened. Believe me, he wasn't a bad seed."

"Are you sure you can talk about it, Ma?"

"I will, but not here." She looked out the window. "Let's take a cab home, shall we, Sara?"

Chapter Eighteen

Back in their kitchen, Helen poured steaming hot chocolate into two mugs. Sara looked around the room, darkened by the storm, and felt the weight of her family's history. The desk with Helen's favorite photos, the clock above the refrigerator showing the noon hour, the broom closet where her mother still kept the rent money that she saved each month to pay Grandma and Poppy. It was here Sara had been fed and frightened, hopeful and horrified. She sensed that her mother was finally about to share the part of her past she had kept hidden all these years.

"Sara, dear, you're not going to be happy with what I tell you."

"It doesn't matter, Ma. If you tell the truth, I need to hear it."

Helen, sitting at the table and sipping her hot chocolate, began. "It was June 1941. Neither your father nor I had diplomas from high school. I had to drop out and go to work because my father came down with pneumonia. He forbade me to see your father because of his truancy. But your father pleaded with me. He told me he'd be enlisting with the Army Corps of Engineers. Before he left, he wanted me with him at the Savoy Ballroom that Saturday. That was June 28, the night he confessed to me he wasn't ready to get married. But he loved me, he said, and wanted to protect me and make sure nothing bad happened to me. He promised we'd be together always and that he'd make a success of his life. I didn't know then that he was already hooked."

"You believed him?"

"Love blinded me. I thought I could help him, save him from making bad choices. I thought we could still have our charmed life together after the war. I thought he'd be over his disappointment. He could make up his courses, if he wanted to, and he could graduate. So I agreed to go to the Savoy with him—and I regretted that night the rest of my life."

Helen got up from the table, filled her hand with tissues, and paced the room. "When we got up to the club, he wanted me…I feel so ashamed."

"What are *you* ashamed of, Ma?"

"God should forgive me." She began tearing her tissues to shreds. "Your father wanted me to…" She was having trouble continuing.

"Do you need some water, Ma?"

"I'll be OK." She sat back down at the table. "The Moonglow dancers had won a citywide competition and were being showcased in the ballroom, the Cats Corner. Al Cooper, the bandleader of the Sultans, asked your father and the Detones to jam with his band. I was so proud of him—but then, when their set ended, your father pulled me toward him and…handed me a skinny cigarette and wanted me to smoke it. He got it from Spencer who was also there. It was weed, reefer…and…I ended up smoking it.

"Then I heard Spencer say to Josef, 'Eednay an ixfay?' Your father said he was talking Pig Latin. 'Spencer wants us to go with him to the Backstage where they have some harder stuff for getting high—some heroin.'"

Helen lifted her head. Her cheeks were flushed. "Your father said, 'Let's you, me, and Spencer go to the Backstage. You'll see, Helen, there's nothing to be afraid of.' I shouted, 'You're crazy! How could you love me and need to do something like that?' I was hysterical. 'Why did you bring me here?' I shouted. 'I don't want to ruin my life. Do you want to destroy me?'"

"So you left Daddy there?"

"I *wish* I left him. But I didn't. Your father said, 'Calm down, Helen. We think for ourselves. We're not fooled by social taboos. Even doctors take heroin. We can handle it.' That crazy Spencer kept egging both of us on, more and more, and I didn't stop him, like I should have. I went, Sara, I went. So that's how I know about heroin, how it feels. I went along with it." Helen's body seemed to crumple into a ball. "And I did it more than once."

Sara was shocked, confused. *My mother? How could it be? If Ma took heroin, had she been addicted, too?* Sara was reeling. She felt nauseated and suddenly chilled.

"*Mamela,*" Helen said. "I was the lucky one. Annette learned that I was sneaking out to the Savoy and going to the Backstage. She told your grandfather about it. He threatened to beat me black and blue. I didn't dare see your father after that. For months, my father punished me, kept all the money I earned on my job for himself. I felt totally bereft, but I later realized I was fortunate. I was able to walk away from drugs and put them behind me. That was it. Some can leave it, Sara, but some cannot. Your father wasn't so lucky as I was. He couldn't stop, even though for years I naively hoped that his willpower and the love he had for us would help him stop.

"I made your father promise me he'd stay clean. I told him I wouldn't ever marry him if he didn't promise me. Maybe he thought he was still in control and could give heroin up if he wanted to. He vowed to me that he'd stop. But he couldn't. Believe it or not, he stayed hooked right into the army, through his overseas service, and all the years you were growing up. I spent my life trying to fix a broken man."

Sara, astonished, didn't know what to say, how to feel. For so many years, she had wanted to know about the past her mother had been withholding, and now that she heard the rest of the story, she didn't know what to do. It was too overwhelming! She stood completely still.

Then, suddenly, surprisingly, she was overcome by a feeling of great relief. *Ma's lived through unbelievably hard times, and she survived!* Sara felt an immense gratitude. She clasped her hands and said spontaneously, "Thank you, thank you, thank you," with tears trickling down her face. She felt a great surge of love for her mother, a great trust in her. At that moment, as if by miracle, the snowplow on Penn Street began flashing orange lights through the kitchen window. It seemed to Sara as if those lights created a halo around her mother's seated figure.

She joined her mother at the table, and put her arms around her again. She wondered where their lives would go from here, now that she and her mother finally had no more secrets between them. She thought about her own future. Was it the right time to tell her mother about her English teacher's encouragement?

In her elation and sense of relief, Sara summoned the courage to share her dream of going to college. "Ma, I'll be graduating in a year. My dream is to go to a good college, maybe Binghamton or Albany."

A nervous energy suddenly filled the kitchen. Helen began fidgeting with her napkin. "Sara, dear, we can't afford for you to go away to college," she said, embarrassment on her face.

"I know the cost is more than we can afford, Ma, with tuition, room and board, and everything. But I'm going to try for a scholarship. Miss Newman thinks I have a good chance of doing well because I'm a good writer."

"It's not just the cost, sweetheart," Helen said, her eyes not meeting Sara's. "The truth is I still need your help at home. Rachel will still be in elementary school. Robbie will be starting high school. I'll be working. I might take an accounting course at Kathryn Gibbs, so I can move out of sales. Without your help, I can't manage all that. Also, we don't know how long Grandma and Poppy will let us keep the apartment. They may even sell the building." Her voice was plaintive, sad. "I wish life was different, so you could have your dream." She began coughing, a raspy, nasty sound.

Sara instantly felt deflated. *How can I even think of abandoning Ma now, going away to college, when she's not able to help herself? I'm more tied to her than ever. But how long do I continue saving her?*

A heavy curtain seemed to descend in front of Sara, separating her from a wide world of promise.

Chapter Nineteen | 1965

Shards of sunlight angled through the basement windows of Eastern District High School's lunchroom, where Sara sat across the table from Ruth. Seniors this semester, they were both taking creative writing.

Sara needed to confide in her friend. They'd already shared so much, but never what really happened to their fathers. *Why? Why haven't I shared my father's secret with Ruth?* Sara picked at her food, then pushed her tray aside. "I rode the Greyhound to Binghamton last week and got into trouble," she said.

"Trouble? Is everything OK with your scholarship?"

"God," Sara moaned, "I hope the mess I made hasn't spread that far." She bit her lip. Sara had won a tuition-free scholarship to the State University at Binghamton. Ruth was still waiting to hear from the United Negro College Fund about her application to Morgan State.

"What happened at Binghamton?"

"I visited Larry Roth. You remember, last year's G.O. president. He's a freshman there. He invited me to come to his Health Education class."

"What's wrong with that?"

"I had an outburst," Sara whispered.

Ruth leaned over the table. "What do you mean? Did you get sick?"

"Larry was...awfully nice. He's a good person."

"Nice about what?"

"His professor was discussing addictions." Sara looked directly at Ruth. "He was talking about methadone, a new drug. I could tell his professor didn't know much. He was actually speaking...*inaccurately*. I can't explain it. I saw red. I ended up insulting the professor." She cleared her throat and looked into Ruth's eyes. "He was being a pompous ass. I just couldn't let it slide."

The concern in Ruth's warm, dark eyes assured Sara of her friend's loyal friendship. Yes, she could trust Ruth. "When my father died...last year...it wasn't a heart attack."

"It wasn't?"

"He died...while he was on methadone. My mother doesn't like me talking about it."

"Your father died...from methadone? I'm so sorry, Sara."

"He didn't exactly die *from* methadone. I don't really know his cause of death. But he died while he was *taking* methadone. My father hated that drug. It doesn't matter why. In any case, I disagreed in class with Larry's teacher—I couldn't control myself. I told him that he should check out what addicts in Harlem had to say before he spread hearsay around as if it were research."

"Oh my! How did Larry react?"

"He was shocked, especially when his teacher got uptight. Larry wrote to me about it." She lifted a letter out of her school bag. "Can I read it to you? I think he's being supportive, but I'm too upset to tell for sure."

Ruth nodded, and Sara read:

> I hope that run-in you had with my Health Education teacher won't turn you against Binghamton. It was unfortunate. I believe you know what you're talking about, and you just wanted to contribute what you knew to the discussion. Hey! You're an honor student. If you say this drug, methadone, has its problems, I don't know why the prof needed to argue with you. He might simply have been surprised that a female, a class visitor, was challenging his praise of a federally supported program. Knowing you, I think you saw him as a chauvinist. You walked out of class, so you must have been really upset. If I'm not being too forward, I think you might consider what to do in the future when you're in a situation like that. Then again, you're probably going to be a writing major where the profs are more liberal, more open to dialogue.

"What do you think, Ruth? Is Larry turned off?"

"Noooo," she said slowly, "I think he's impressed with your assertiveness and likes you a lot. Some men," she said rolling her eyes, "appreciate women who speak up."

There weren't many teenage girls at Eastern District who, like Sara, were attracted to feminism, but Ruth, who had overcome her shyness and won Eastern District's Good Citizen's Award, was someone Sara could talk to about women's roles. Sara had always admired Ruth's mother, Angela. Like Helen, Angela was supporting three children on her own by holding down two jobs.

"I don't think I've ever told you, Sara, about my father. Why he's not living with us. He cheated on my mother, and she chased him out," Ruth continued. "She didn't want to be a doormat. So, to my mother, my father's as dead as yours."

Sara digested Ruth's revelation. "Is your mom seeing anyone else?"

"No. She doesn't want any boyfriends."

"My mom's seeing a man now," Sara said.

"Really? Do you like him?"

"Not really. Not much at all."

"Why not?"

"He has young kids and wants my mom to marry him."

"You don't need to say anything more."

The poster Sara admired was still on Mrs. Rifkin's office door—Martin Luther King Jr. delivering his "I Have a Dream Speech" in Washington, D.C.

"Sara! I'm happy to see you. Congratulations on winning the scholarship to Binghamton. I meant to ask you to come by."

"Thank you, Mrs. Rifkin. I didn't realize you knew."

"News like yours travels fast in this the school," Mrs. Rifkin said with a laugh.

Mrs. Rifkin glanced down at her schedule book, then up again at Sara. "Would you like to talk? I have some time left on my lunch hour."

"But you're still eating," Sara said, noticing half of a tuna sandwich on Mrs. Rifkin's desk.

Mrs. Rifkin placed the rest of her lunch in her lunch bag. "A snack for later. Come sit down."

Sara sat on the familiar couch. "Actually, Mrs. Rifkin, my going to Binghamton has brought up some problems."

"Oh? I remember you telling me that your mother objected to your going out of town..."

"As it turns out, my mother's come around. She'd prefer me to stay at home, but she's not as dependent on me anymore. She's seeing someone...a man she might marry."

Mrs. Rifkin took a moment to think. "Has it been about a year since your father died?"

"Too short of a time!" Sara blurted out. "I'm not taking too well to this new man. I'm suspicious of his motives. His wife died, and he told my mother he never really loved his wife. Their marriage had been arranged when they were children in Hungary. I can imagine what it must have been like for his wife, being married to a man who didn't love her."

"How does he treat your mother?" Mrs. Rifkin asked.

"He puts her on a pedestal. Wines and dines her. Says my mother is his true love! But like I said, I'm suspicious. He has kids of his own, three of them, who still need mothering. I'm afraid my mother will be saddled with more children, just when she wanted greater independence." Sara took a deep breath.

"Is this problem connected to Binghamton?"

Sara smiled with embarrassment. "No. Please forgive me. I'm here because of what happened when I visited Larry Roth. You remember him from the G.O.? He's at Binghamton now. I insulted his Health Education teacher who was talking about a drug my father used to take. The professor became angry. I lost control, disagreed with him inappropriately, and stormed out of his class. I'm thoroughly ashamed of how I acted."

"What made you so upset?" Mrs. Rifkin leaned forward in her chair.

"I know it's connected to my feelings about my father. I still can't figure out why my father had to die." Teary-eyed, Sara looked up at Mrs. Rifkin. "He was so young—only forty-two. I know addiction is hard to overcome, but some people are able to do it. Why couldn't he? Why didn't he find proper support? Was it just not available? Or did his ego get in the way? I tried to talk to my mother about this. She believes that some addicts are able to quit, and some are not. For some people, no matter what they try, the dependency becomes permanent."

"You want to understand your father better, but he's not alive for you to talk to him," Mrs. Rifkin said sympathetically.

"Exactly," Sara said.

There was a short silence between them.

"You're a good writer," Mrs. Rifkin said earnestly. "Why don't you try writing about your father's last day? I mean, really envision that last day. Imagine his thoughts and feelings. You'd be surprised how much understanding you can get when you imagine what another person is thinking and feeling."

"I never really talked much with my father. Not as much as I wanted to." A long-standing, wrenching guilt rose up in her. "Not as much as I should have."

"But you lived with him, spent time with him. Why don't you give it a try? You can even write directly to him, if you want to, as in a letter." She gathered some folders before her on the desk. "I have some guidelines here for writing to a deceased parent. I wrote them myself because it happens so often. A parent dies before a student has the chance to say goodbye. Would you care to look these over?"

"Yes, Mrs. Rifkin. I'd like that."

"I wish I could talk more now, but I have appointments," she said apologetically. "Let's set something up for tomorrow morning before your classes begin. How's that?"

"Good, Mrs. Rifkin, very good. I'll see what I can do."

She gave Sara a hug and told her she was really glad that Sara had come to see her again.

"Of course," Sara gulped, her anxiety mounting as she imagined herself writing about her father's death. It was one thing for Mrs. Rifkin to suggest that she write about his last day, but quite another for her to put herself through the pain again by writing all her feelings down. She had lived in dread of her father's behavior and experienced her family's break-up firsthand. Her head was full of contradictory emotions—fear, disappointment, anger, guilt. How could writing help? She'd read the guidelines.

Dear Dad,

Toward the end of your life, I blamed you for leaving us in Williamsburg and for moving in with Grandma and Poppy in Queens. You appeared to be caving in to what Grandma Hannah wanted. Of course, you also had pity on her because she watched her first son, your brother, die. And she developed a debilitating case of arthritis. She thought that because you couldn't end your twenty-five-year heroin addiction, the only thing that would make you quit would be losing us.

As I'm writing this, I realize that Mom and I, not only you, allowed Grandma to direct us. I always loved Grandma Hannah and wanted to please her. She told me when I was eight years old that if only I would ask you to end your habit, which was ruining our family, you'd listen to me because I was your darling little girl. I can still hear her words, though I realize now how impossible her idea was. I was just a child.

Grandma and Poppy were willing to spend any amount of money to help cure you, so Mom was willing to endure the rough periods, even your hurting her at times, when you were desperate for money. I can't believe I watched you hit her! But Mom had hopes there was a cure, until all the options Grandma Hannah paid for came to nothing. I remember you going through cold turkey at Veterans Hospital in Lexington, Kentucky, when I was eight and a half, and I thought you were going to die. I watched you sink into depression after having shock therapy at Hawthorne Lodge. I was ten then, and I felt very sorry for you. And then you dragged Mom off to Florida, at Grandma's urging. You were gone so long, and I felt so alone. But you didn't get better. In fact, you got worse, and you took Mom down with you! How could you? You became too sick even to put in a day's work. And still, I wanted to save you—save you through my words. I wished

I could have spoken to you, Dad. That's when Grandma Hannah stepped in for good. And we let her. How she convinced you to leave us—and how she prevented Mom from resisting—these things still bewilder and anger me. And so, I blamed you for letting Grandma control you. I know she meant well, but we saw her as coldhearted. I feel sorry for the shame you must have suffered. It makes me ache to remember the day you left. I don't know if I can go on telling this story about your last days, because it hurts so much. And there are so many gaps in what I know. Yet I feel I have to continue writing as a way of easing my mind, even if I have to fill in from my imagination whatever I don't truly know.

Shortly after you moved in with Grandma and Poppy in Little Neck, you reluctantly began the methadone program in Harlem. You said you had no choice. Who knows? Grandma may have even threatened to tell the police about your habit and turn you in to the prison on Riker's Island or readmit you to Lexington Hospital. At least you visited us on Sundays. How we missed you the rest of the week! I know you didn't like Dr. Barish's personality—I heard you rant to Mom about his delusions of grandeur and his need for control—but taking methadone helped you go back to work with Uncle Irv. But on some days, you were too ill to work. You'd visit the clinic so that Dr. Barish could adjust your dosages of methadone. On good days, though, you were fully responsible for your Manhattan deliveries, just as you were in the past.

Though I believe that you, a grown man, a father, felt humiliated living with your parents, I think your Sunday visits with us made you feel better and gave you hope that one day soon you'd be reunited with us. You told Mom you were off heroin and wanted our family to move to Long Island where Robbie, Rachel, and I would have better schools and parks. You were earning a good living again, and you told Mom she would be able to stop working. You said it didn't matter if Grandma and Poppy thought your return to us was premature. You needed to be with us! We all wanted to hear that. Ma thought it was too good to be true. I still remember Ma's words to you over the phone that Sunday, when you pleaded with her to take you back: "Yes, Josef, I want us all to be together, but you have to be the old Josef again. You need to be the man I used to know, the man with ambition and hope, before you became so…so…negative." Ma told me you promised her you *were* that man, and she said to you, "We'll see."

Do you remember that, Dad? Ma thought your addiction had weakened you and caused you to give in to Grandma's influence too easily, and now she wanted to be sure you were strong again. She needed to be certain that you could stay free of drugs and that you could stand up for yourself in the face of Grandma's pressure. Was she right, Dad?

I wish I knew what happened to you on that Sunday when you never made it home to see us. Could it be that you didn't feel well that December morning when you left Grandma and Poppy in Little Neck? Did you drive up to the methadone clinic in Harlem to have Dr. Barish check your dosage? You must have known that an overdose of methadone could be lethal.

Oh, Dad, when will I stop blaming you for not giving up heroin totally? Mom has tried to show me that addiction had you in its claws and being hooked meant you lost control over yourself. But I guess on some level I believed you, when I heard you say, "I'll stop whenever I'm good and ready." I have never given up my childish wish that when you said that, you really *did* have the power to save your life. And if you really did have the power to save your life, but you didn't use that power, then I concluded you just didn't love *us* enough to save yourself. I felt so rejected!

I imagine you on December 21, 1963, the day you died. And here is where I have to fill in things I'm not sure about. While you're on your way to Williamsburg to check on Poppy's butcher shop before heading to see us on Penn

Street, you feel so ill that you decide to stop by Dr. Barish's clinic. You explain to Dr. Barish that you're feeling weak and woozy. You wonder, if by some mistake, you've received the wrong dosage. I hear Dr. Barish tell you brashly that a mistake would have been impossible because the dosages in every bottle are measured exactly, and I hear his accusing words: "Mr. Katz, you must have helped *yourself* to an extra dosage!" You may have responded that you'd never take extra methadone because that would be suicide. And then, Dr. Barish may have told you to take a urine test. I picture him reading the results and calling you a liar, refusing to treat you any further as a patient, and phoning for an ambulance because you were in grave danger. Maybe my imagination is running away with me, but given what I've heard you say about Dr. Barish, such a scene seems possible. I hear you calling Barish a charlatan as you rush out of the clinic.

I hear Barish shout back at you, "Mr. Katz! You need treatment!"

I can imagine how frightened you must have been. Maybe you began to doubt you would ever get better. I see you sitting in the Cadillac you loved, parked near the clinic. As you think about our family, a snakelike chain begins to twist around your neck. Will Mom accept your proposal to reunite as a family or will she altogether refuse you? And if she agrees to get back together, can you really afford a house in the suburbs? Can you tolerate the drive back and forth each day into Manhattan? Can you be in Manhattan and stay clean? How overwhelmed you must have felt. I see you start the engine of your car, drive south along the East River, and head toward to Williamsburg.

When you reach Grand Street, I imagine you overcome by one of your bouts of nausea. You have to get off the road and stop the car. Your nearness to Greenwich Village, where you used to buy drugs, brings on the memory of heroin's euphoria. You know the methadone in your system will reduce the ecstasy of a heroin high, but taking enough heroin will bring ample pleasure. Maybe you feel the torture of that painful moment—to resist, or slip back; to turn away, or to use…

You pull the Cadillac to the curb in front of your father's butcher shop on Bedford Avenue. You stand before the storefront window and observe your reflection in the glass—your tired face, the dark, hollow bags under your eyes. You think it's not too late to get your old spunk back.

You enter Poppy's store and lock the door behind you. It's been a week since you've been in his shop. The store looks pretty much as you saw it last, though you want your father to know that his man, Bob, hasn't been doing a good job of sweeping up the sawdust. Meat counters on the left are cleared; wooden benches on the right are in place; white porcelain walls trimmed in blue are wiped clean. There's no way, you think, to rid the front of the store of the sweet smell of fatty lamb, even though the long racks with big hooks on the walls are completely clean and empty.

I see you advance to the rear counter, flip it up, pass the four-legged butcher block where you used to slice brisket, and move through the narrow hallway into the back room. You sit on a wooden stool and think about your life: *Helen should never have told my mother about my problem. The whole family pushed me into treatment when I wasn't ready to stop. Those quack doctors at Lexington didn't have a clue. Those phoneys! They sent me to Clayton, the hypocrite psychiatrist. And Hawthorne Lodge almost destroyed my mind. And who needs Barish, that bastard! I can stop on my own. I have the power. I'm the one in charge.*

Suddenly, you feel chilled and your body starts to shake. You step into the bathroom and pull the string for light. You sit on the toilet bowl, fold your arms around your chest to warm yourself, and nod off for a few moments. Suddenly the room begins to swim in circles around your head. You feel the tremors, your lips turning blue. How terrified you must have felt! You get up, pace back and forth in the little room. You're so dizzy that you fall to the floor. You're having trouble breathing; you begin to gurgle. You reach for the sink, pull yourself up, and find the small wax paper bag in the depth of your pocket.

Where did that bag of heroin come from? I've asked myself that question so many times. Did you get it when you stopped on Grand Street? Did you already have it in your pocket when you started out that morning? Did you have it because you needed to prove to yourself you could resist the urge? Or because you might come to the point when you could resist no longer?

And this next part is the hardest part for me to imagine—the hardest to put into words. This is when Grandma's words to me as an eight-year-old repeat themselves in my head: "You have to tell your daddy to stop. He'll do it for you."

You rest the small bag on top of the toilet and take a metal soup spoon and a pack of matches from a shelf in the cabinet. You bend the stem of the spoon back so that it resembles the handle of a teacup, pick up the bag of white powder, and spread it carefully onto the spoon. After using a toothpick to mix the powder with a drop or two of water and lighting a match to heat and dissolve the solution carefully so as not to spill a precious drop, you absorb the mixture. You use one of your mother's hypodermic needles Poppy keeps in the cabinet in case Grandma might feel faint when she's in the shop and needs insulin. Then you do what you have done so many times before. You strap your belt tightly around your forearm and try to find an unused vein. You pump the syringe in your arm in and out, close your eyes, and wait for the rush.

Finally, Daddy, I understand. Your aloneness. Your feeling no one can really help. Your deep, deep need, and then your total loss of control. I understand now that no one could stop you at the moment when you were seized by addiction; it was impossible. Impossible, too, I finally realize, for me, as a little girl, to turn your addiction around. But I'm not little now, and I have to tell you that I understand how your confidence as a man must have been chipped away, not only by your sickness and people's ignorance, but also by all our family's unwise choices. I understand your feeling that you needed to save face, so you denied what was really happening.

I want you to know, Daddy, what I've decided to do with my life. In a few months, I'll be graduating from high school. I've won a scholarship to the University of New York at Binghamton, and Mom's letting me live away from home. I want to major in writing. Someday I hope to write a book about the terrible effects of heroin addiction, especially on the wives of addicts. You loved fairness and justice, and I want to work toward those ideals, especially for women. I believe Mom when she says you wanted to make her happy, and I hope, Dad, that I will make you proud.

Epilogue | 2016

When I reflect today on Sara's life, which is based on my own, I think about the choices I've made that were influenced by my father's addiction. As author, I granted Sara more freedom than I had. Sara lived her dream of going away to college after her father died because she earned a scholarship, whereas in real life, I stayed at home after my father's death and lived with my mom, brother, and sister. I attended a city college in my neighborhood, where tuition was then twenty-four dollars a credit, which was all we could afford.

But my emotional ties to my mother also prevented me from leaving home, even if I could have afforded it. My family was in turmoil, but one thing was certain. As the oldest child who had witnessed my mother's experience of physical and emotional bullying by my father, I internalized a deep sense of responsibility for her and my younger siblings. I couldn't leave them behind! We had gone through family trauma together, and that experience bonded us strongly. The bonds with my siblings remain, though our lives have gone in different directions.

At the end of the narrative, Sara is about to graduate from high school when she writes a letter to her deceased father, a victim of heroin overdose. Sara's last words to him are forgiving; she wants him to be proud of her in college and beyond. However, in real life, I didn't fully forgive my father until I had gone through the long process of writing extensively about my past, a process of continual revision that lasted thirty years.

When I began this effort, I used the conventional form of memoir, writing in the first person. I characterized my father more negatively then—as selfish, irresponsible, and immature. It was one of two different pictures of my father that my mother had painted when he was alive. One picture depicted him as incapable of being a proper father because his heroin habit dominated his life. That picture of him filled me with rage and kept me bogged down in anger and self-pity for having been born into a family with a heroin-addicted father. The other portrait my mother painted illustrated all the positive reasons she stayed loyal to him throughout their marriage until his death at age forty-two.

What was missing then was a fuller understanding of what my father was really up against. He had been addicted for close to thirty years by the time he died. In the 1950s, when my family tried to force him to find a cure—against his will—the available methods were expensive and ineffective. I remember my father hoping that addictive drugs, not only methadone but also heroin, would eventually become legalized, so he could benefit from medical maintenance of his condition. Though we have seen the legalization of marijuana in some parts of our country and around the world, discussions of legalization have not extended to heroin, and the black-market industry that supplies heroin illegally has grown to a trillion dollars.

Obsessive academic achievement was my way of escaping from depression and grief. I was bent on proving by my success that I was worthy of the love my father hadn't shown to me. When I was a junior in college, I met my first husband. Although he was bright and politically progressive, he held one temporary job after another. He was older than I and had dropped out of college several times. I was attracted to him because he showed me love and physical attention, and I thought I could help him graduate from college. I didn't recognize then that I was following the same pattern my mother had set: marrying a man who was wounded in a certain way and assuming the role of caretaker to help him regain his pride and productivity. We married after I thought I was pregnant.

At that time, I was drawn to the Women's Liberation Movement. The consciousness-raising meetings I attended in different women's Manhattan and Brooklyn apartments helped me see that women were being socialized to heal men's ailments, and men's treatment of women as sex objects were social problems, not just my own private experience. What was, in fact, "normal" were the problems hundreds, maybe thousands, of women had with men who were enjoying the privilege of having wives.

After seven years of marriage during which my husband continued taking various temporary jobs and pursuing his hobbies while I was the steady breadwinner teaching college English, I felt I needed to leave my marriage in order to preserve my sense of self. By that time, my love of women's literature and student-centered teaching put me at odds with the traditional English departments where I was teaching. With the division of assets that resulted from our divorce, I made the good decisions to undergo therapy and return to graduate school. My goal was to teach in the interdisciplinary field of Women's Studies that was growing around the country.

The flowering field of women's literature inspired me to write my memoir as a novel, following the advice of Virginia Woolf. In her famous essay *A Room of One's Own*, Woolf made several points that applied to me. She believed that women couldn't find their authentic writing voices if they wrote in angry defiance, because anger causes writers to be stuck on themselves rather than on their subjects. She believed fiction was a genre enabling women writers to remove themselves to a significant degree from personal injuries and resentments and reach essential truths that moved beyond the mere facts.

I realized that if I wrote my story as fiction rather than as a memoir, I would need to find the good and the strong in all the major figures who shaped my painful childhood—not only my father, but also my mother and grandmother. Novels require well-rounded characters because human beings are multidimensional, with many complicated sides to their personalities. I therefore credit my mother for sharing with me the attractive sides of my father's personality that drew her to him in the 1930s—qualities she continued to see in him even as he struggled, and failed, to overcome his addiction. I admire her strength in keeping our family together without demonizing the man who could have turned into a total monster in my child-eyes. My mother's persistent hope, living side by side with her anger, that our situation could improve enabled me to remember all the good things that happened to me under my father's influence. My relationship with my mother improved after her short-lived second marriage ended in annulment. In a little less than a year, the financial success her new husband claimed to have proved fraudulent, and my mother and I were able to provide true emotional support for each other, openly discussing life's ups and downs.

My sister and brother helped bring about my ability to forgive my grandmother. My sister was seven when our father died, and she knew of him only as being sick, not addicted. When he passed on, she thought our grandmother was the one trying to nurse our father back to health. When our father was still alive, my brother spent time with him and our grandfather in their respective butcher shops, watching them cut meat and helping them serve customers. When my brother got his driver's license, he sometimes worked for our grandfather delivering meat and poultry to customers. Occasionally my brother would visit with Grandma after hours, when our grandfather returned home.

Neither my sister's nor my brother's breach with our grandmother was as great as my mother's and mine. Though my mother's relationship with my grandmother unfortunately remained strained, my feelings shifted when I learned Grandma had been placed in a nursing home because she had Alzheimer's and was getting violent, even with Poppy. I felt I had to visit her.

I went to the nursing home with my aunt (my father's sister) and her family, with whom my grandparents had been living. I remember seeing my grandmother sitting up in bed, staring into space with an angry look on her face. "Hello, Grandma. It's Sharon," I said. Her stare, direct and piercing, remained unchanged. I looked more deeply into her eyes. "I'm your granddaughter, Grandma. Georgie's little girl. Do you remember Georgie?" I saw something there in her eyes. Something flickered. Was it terror, recognition, sorrow? I remembered how her eyes had flashed with fire when I was eight years old and she told me that my father would listen to me because I was his little girl, and he would never do anything to hurt me. I thought at that moment about what it must have been like for her to lose two sons. I took my grandmother's hand. It was cold, and I tried to warm it in my hands. I felt my anger subside. I kissed her cheek and said goodbye. I forgave her, finally, and both my mother and I resumed a relationship with my grandfather after Grandma died.

Now that I am seventy years old, married to a sensitive and loving man, and retired from teaching, I've been in a twelve-step program for a year. In the process of finishing my novel, I realized that part of my family's problem was our secretiveness and isolation. Personal reflection and therapy did not enable me to see my situation as a child of a heroin addict in the same kind of social terms that I had come to understand my position as a woman. It took belonging to a twelve-step community for me to understand the ways heroin addiction affected other women and men.

I wish my father had had the benefit of twelve-step teachings—teachings that view substance abuse as an illness that causes brain dysfunction. Such a view encourages those who are addicts and the people affected by them to come forward and reach out for help, instead of feeling shame because of their problems.

In my case, the shame was exacerbated by being raised Jewish. Jewish communities often deny that addiction occurs within them, and addicts are often stigmatized and shunned. The move to coordinate twelve-step values with the precepts of Judaism (started by Rabbi Abraham Twerski) have helped to pave the way for addiction recovery, which in twelve steps means total abstinence. Perhaps someday my father's vision will also be realized. Perhaps someday it will be possible for addicted users of heroin to participate in legalized medical maintenance programs combined with competent counseling.

I have decided to publish my "fiction"—what the twelve steps calls my "personal inventory"— in the hopes that those who haven't had personal experience with heroin addiction can empathize with the Katz family's predicament, and those who have been affected by addiction can feel the worth of sharing one's story. The twelve steps teach that addiction is a family trauma that affects the behaviors of the addict and those close to the addict. How can children, like myself, deal with the hurtful experiences of having an addicted parent? How can the consequences not be permanently damaging? Had I been part of a twelve-step program earlier in my adult life, I might have overcome the fears I had about being a properly caring parent. I was too afraid that, as a parent, I would recreate a dysfunctional situation similar to the one I had experienced.

For me, it's been a liberating experience to face the past as squarely as I could manage, share my experience with others in meetings, and prepare to have my story published. My message echoes a twelve-step precept: I hope my readers will see that there is no situation so dismal that a community of loving and understanding people cannot help them find a better way out.

Acknowledgments

I am indebted to my constant, excellent editor, Milton Teichman. I owe my progress moving from early drafts to final revision to writing coaches Kathleen Spivack and Steve Joseph. The outstanding guidance and kindness of Claudia Volkman, editor at KiCam Projects, brought professional refinement to my manuscript. My colleague-writers in writing groups on Cape Cod and in Oaxaca have been essential affirmers and editors: Lesley Gordon, Cheryl Dockser, Elaine Alford, Tonia St. Germain, on the Cape; Susana Wald, Alice Jennings, Pierre Sollier, Joy McCalister, Ida and Don Watanabe, and Carol Hobart in Oaxaca. The San Miguel writing community has encouraged my process, including author/editor Lynda Schor. Additional readers of my full manuscript have my deep gratitude and admiration: Barbara Moore, Sheila Eidelman, Bobbi Salisch, Arline Lowenthal, and Jessica Shapiro. I wish especially to acknowledge my sister, Devorah Vidal, not only for leading me to the twelve steps by her shining example but for sharing her truths about our family at every stage of my writing process.

About the Author

Sharon Leder taught English, women's studies, and Jewish studies on several campuses of the State University of New York and is Associate Professor Emerita at S.U.N.Y.-Nassau Community College. As a teacher, she wrote books and articles on women writers, on the literature of the Holocaust, and on women in academia before beginning the second half of her life as a fiction writer and poet. An earlier draft of her novel *The Fix* was a finalist in Merrimack Media's Outstanding Writer Award (2015). Several of Leder's short works of fiction have been anthologized or published online. In her fiction, Leder uses her life story as the oldest daughter of a heroin addict to help her imagine ways for her characters to survive conflict, tragedy, and trauma without losing sight of the supports they need to prevail. As an adult in the ongoing process of recovery, she has been helped by twelve-step programs, nonprofit groups that stress self-help in the context of loving community. Leder resides on Cape Cod with her husband, artist and author Milton Teichman. Together they run The Teichman Art Gallery. Visit Leder at www.SharonLeder.com